Praise from Students
for Leslie Bowman's *Online Learning*

"This excellent resource, with easy-to-understand tables and tips, will ensure success for every level of online learner. Nothing is left out. While the chapters on 'Tips to Getting Started' and 'Common Mistakes to Avoid' put to rest fears and confusion for the novice student, the advanced learner will also find insights to make their learning experience more successful. A definite must-read for every online student!" —**Christina Mazmanian**, online graduate student

"This book will serve any student who desires success. The pitfalls of procrastination cannot be stressed enough, and the author reiterates commitment to time and organization throughout. Once a student adopts some of the strategies for time management and organization, the better grades just happen. The information in this manual is well suited to guiding the student toward choices that lead to success." —**Kenneth Coats**, online student (graduated)

"While *Online Learning* is specifically geared toward preparing individuals interested in starting an online program, it is an excellent resource that would benefit all students and increase their academic success. It appeals to all types of learners and gives step-by-step suggestions to increase the effectiveness of study skills in order to obtain and maintain outstanding grades. Why limit this resource to online learning applicants? It is a must-read for the success of today's students, both online and in the classrooms." —**Suzzette Mc-Clean**, online student (graduated)

"Even though I have taken over twenty online classes, I still picked up good ideas. For the new online student, my advice is: Get this book!" —**Gregg Sadler**, online student (graduated)

ONLINE LEARNING

A USER-FRIENDLY APPROACH FOR HIGH SCHOOL AND COLLEGE STUDENTS

Leslie Bowman

ROWMAN & LITTLEFIELD EDUCATION

A division of
Rowman & Littlefield Publishers, Inc.
Lanham • New York • Toronto • Plymouth, UK

Published by Rowman & Littlefield Education
A division of Rowman & Littlefield Publishers, Inc.
A wholly owned subsidiary of The Rowman & Littlefield Publishing Group, Inc.
4501 Forbes Boulevard, Suite 200, Lanham, Maryland 20706
http://www.rowmaneducation.com

Estover Road, Plymouth PL6 7PY, United Kingdom

British Library Cataloguing in Publication Information Available

Library of Congress Cataloging-in-Publication Data

Bowman, Leslie, 1955-
  Online learning : a user-friendly approach for high school and college
students / Leslie Bowman.
    p. cm.
  Includes bibliographical references.
  ISBN 978-1-60709-747-1 (cloth : alk. paper) — ISBN 978-1-60709-749-5
(electronic)
  1. Education, Higher--Computer-assisted instruction. 2. Education—Effect of
technological innovations on. 3. Educational technology—United States.
4. Web-based instruction. I. Title.
  LB2395.7.B68 2010
  378.1'7344678—dc22
                                                    2010006481

♾™ The paper used in this publication meets the minimum requirements of
American National Standard for Information Sciences—Permanence of Paper
for Printed Library Materials, ANSI/NISO Z39.48-1992.
Manufactured in the United States of America.

Printed in the United States of America

In memory of my colleague and friend Tom,
whose ideas, encouragement, and support
went far beyond his contribution to this book.

This book is dedicated to
all new and lifelong online learners
and the professionals who teach them.

CONTENTS

ACKNOWLEDGMENTS

I have met so many wonderful online teachers, students, and colleagues over the years that I could not possibly begin to name them all. Yet each, in his or her own way, has contributed much to my knowledge and experience in this field.

The book chapter contributors are experienced and dedicated online learners and teachers. They are highly regarded in their respective professional fields. I am honored to include their contributions to this book for beginning online learners.

Some people believe that online friendships and professional support are not as strong as those we make in our "real" lives. To the contrary, I have found that my online friends and colleagues provide personal and professional support far beyond the boundaries of geographic location. Thank you to all my online friends and colleagues around the world.

INTRODUCTION

In every online class, some students are wildly successful, some earn average or slightly below average grades, some barely pass, some fail, and some drop out. Whether you are a new or experienced online student, whatever your age and background, everything you need to know about successfully completing an online class is right here in your hands.

You may be a high school student, a twenty-something college student, a working adult returning to school after many years, or a single parent going to college for the first time. You may be a computer genius or you may be completely computer illiterate. Maybe you are a traditional high school or college student who does not want to take online classes, but you are forced into online learning because your school building has closed due to a natural disaster.

Whatever your reasons, going to school online will fit into your personal and professional lifestyle better than going to a campus classroom if (and that is a *big* if) you are properly prepared for the online learning experience.

Whatever your age, situation, or lifestyle, you can be successful in your online class. The primary reasons students fail or drop out of online classes are that they are unprepared for how much time they will need to spend studying each week and they are not organized for online learning. Most students find that once they understand the first and learn how to do the second, they can be quite success-ful in online classes.

Some students ask if they are smart enough to take an online class. I have known students who wanted good grades without put-ting forth any effort. I have also known students who could not make it because they didn't schedule the necessary time to do their work. I've had students who, for various reasons, were not success-ful. Truthfully, though, I've never had a student who was not "smart enough."

With rare exceptions, anyone can make good grades in an online class. Making good grades in an online class is not about being "smart enough" to do the work. Making good grades is all about planning and managing time to get the work done without rush-ing through everything at the very last minute. The more time students spend on class work, the better grades they will make in online classes.

WHY TAKE AN ONLINE CLASS?

People decide to enroll in an online class for many reasons, the pri-mary one being convenience. Going to campus to attend class means making sure you're on time when class starts and staying until class is over. Going to campus means fighting traffic and weather, finding a parking place, trudging into the building carrying all those books and notebooks and a laptop, hoping you are not the last one to walk into the classroom and that you can still get a seat in the back of the room.

In regular classes on campus, students are often preoccupied with thoughts of work and home. So instead of focusing on lectures, they are thinking about what needs to be done at home, wonder-ing if the baby is coming down with a cold, hoping the babysitter doesn't mind staying a bit late tonight, making mental grocery lists, and various other distractions. Students nod off during lectures, get bored, wonder if they can do the work, hope they will not forget their homework, worry because they did not read the chapters before class, and fear they will look stupid if they can't answer a question in class or on a test.

Somewhere around halfway through the class period, students begin hoping that the professor will let everyone go a little early. Whether the class period is one hour or four hours, during the last half of the class period people are watching the clock and mentally willing the time to go faster.

Sound familiar? I've been there, too, as both a student and a professor. When I taught classes on campus, by the time 9:00 p.m. rolled around and we had been in class since 6:30 and still had an hour to go, eyes would glaze over, the wiggling and fidgeting would start, and students would slump further and further down in the chairs or over the tables. When that last hour or two rolled around, everyone had difficulty focusing after a very long day.

WHAT ARE THE REAL DIFFERENCES?

Taking a class online is a different story entirely. There are only two major differences between going to class on campus and taking a class online. Once students address those differences, they find that online learning is no more difficult than going to class on campus.

The first major difference is that students have to do a lot more reading and writing in an online class than in a campus class. Think about it for a minute. In a campus class, students listen and talk, and neither of those activities takes any appreciable time or energy. On the other hand, in an online class, students write what they want to say and post it as a message in a classroom discussion board. That takes more time than just opening your mouth and blurting out whatever pops into your head.

During discussions in a campus classroom, students listen to what their classmates and professors say. In an online class, students have to read what everyone else has written. Reading takes more time and energy than listening.

The second major difference is that students are alone with the computer rather than sitting in a room with classmates and a professor. Many new online students think that they will feel isolated without having other students around. Some new online students think that they will not be able to get their work done without someone to hold them accountable.

That "someone" usually translates into the "professor." The error there is that campus students have far less access to their professors than online students do. Online professors generally answer questions five or more days a week, while campus professors answer questions in class and during office hours. Those who invite email questions generally only check emails during office hours.

WHAT IS ACCOUNTABILITY?

Accountability is taking responsibility for doing what you should do or need to do and suffering the consequences for failure to do it. Students are responsible for completing assignments on time. No one can make you do the work. Professors do not own that responsibility. It is true that some people find it more difficult to look a professor in the eye and make excuses for not completing their homework than to just pop off an email. Maybe this is what people mean when they say that they need to have someone hold them accountable for doing their work.

You are responsible, whether you go to class and physically hand your work to the professor or whether you send a file electronically. "I need to see my professor every week" is an excuse rather than a reason for not taking online classes.

WON'T I FEEL ISOLATED IN THE ONLINE CLASS?

Isolation is a very real concern for online students. Most people enjoy and need the social element of learning, and the lack of the social element can negatively affect their academic performance. However, online classes, just like regular classes, usually include plenty of interaction with classmates and the professor.

Some schools require the professors to have "live" office hours on the computer in a class chat room or on Instant Messenger. Some schools require professors to have "calling" hours when students can call them on the phone. There are also schools that require neither "on call" hours nor computer "office hours." Even if calling or Instant Messenger hours are not available in an online class, professors are available daily through email and a Q&A area in the online classroom.

Professors and students alike have a role in ensuring that no one feels isolated in an online class. Students need to interact through class and group discussions, and professors have to make their presence known throughout every week in the online class. Unlike regular classes where students can sit back and say nothing for the entire class period, everyone in the online classroom has a responsibility to communicate effectively on an ongoing basis. Because of this ongoing interaction, no one is left out in the cold in an online class, unless it is by individual choice.

WHAT'S NEXT?

The simple answer is to read this book from cover to cover! I will take you step-by-step through the process of getting ready for your first online class, and I will show you how to make sure your work gets done well and on time and how to maintain motivation right up through the last week of the class.

Sitting in class is easy. Sitting at home in front of a computer is easy. What you do while you're sitting in either place determines the level of success you will experience in your classes. In a regular class, you can sit in the back and stay quiet or even snooze, or you can sit in the front and be actively involved in the learning activities. The same is true in the online classroom. Your level of participation and active engagement in the learning activities directly affects the grade you will earn in any class.

HOW DOES THIS BOOK HELP?

Each chapter in this book covers a specific element of online learning and provides the new online student with practical strategies and "how to" information so that any student can go into an online classroom prepared to succeed. Read this book from cover to cover before taking your first online class.

Then after you have started your first class, use this as a reference tool whenever you have questions or run into problems. You can develop self-directed learning skills that will help you become secure and knowledgeable about technology, studying, communicating online, and getting work done on time. If you want to make As in your online classes, then this book is for you.

This book has strategies and tips that every online professor wants students to know before they sign up for an online class. Professors want each and every student to be successful. Professors want students to do their work on time, do it right, interact with classmates, learn new information, and enjoy the entire process of learning. When it comes to succeeding in school, professors can only do so much to help students learn. Students have to be willing and able to take responsibility for their own learning.

WHO AM I, AND HOW DO I KNOW ALL THIS?

I am your online professor. I teach 100 to 150 online students at any given time throughout the year. I have also been an online student. I have taught thousands of online students in the past twelve years, and I can tell you how to make As in your online classes.

Three of my close colleagues have contributed chapters to this book. Two of them are former students of mine in an online graduate program. We have all been brand-new online learners, and we know what it takes to be a successful online student. We will, through each chapter of this book, teach you what we all learned about how to avoid failing or dropping out of an online class.

If you're ready to find out what every online professor wants online students to know, just turn the page and we'll get started.

Welcome to the new and wonderful world of online learning.

1

HOW DOES IT WORK?

TYPES OF ONLINE CLASSES

There are three basic types of online classes: independent study or correspondence courses, synchronous courses, and asynchronous courses. There are also several combinations of these. You will need to determine what kind of learning you prefer and then locate classes that suit your preference.

Independent Study or Correspondence Courses

Independent study or correspondence courses are not formal classes, but rather are course materials that are available to students via print or online. Students sign up and pay for a course, and then the materials are sent one of two ways. One method is for students to receive all materials through postal mail or email. The other method is for students to receive password-protected access to the materials online. In such courses, the work is completed and returned to the professor in the same manner in which the students received the course materials.

These courses work in a variety of ways; in each, students have a certain period of time in which to complete all the course work. Sometimes this is three to six months, or even up to a year. Some professors require that only one assignment be submitted at a time; then the student must wait for the grade and feedback to be returned before another assignment can be submitted. In some courses, the student completes all the work for the course and then sends it to the professor all at once.

This type of course has advantages and disadvantages. The primary advantage is that students can complete the work any time that is convenient during the timeframe of the course, from enrollment to the end date. Students may contact the professor by phone or email if they have questions about the assignments.

Another advantage is that students can move along through the course materials at their own pace. Some students like to complete a course in just a few weeks. Some students like to take their time, completing one assignment per week and thus spending only a few hours a week on their course work.

The primary disadvantage is that procrastination can all too often mean that the course is just never completed. Many students enroll in these types of courses, forget to do the work, and then get a notice that the course end date is in a week. At that point, it's simply too late to do all the work in time.

Another disadvantage is that if the student sends all the course work at the same time, then there is no feedback from the professor. If an assignment is completed incorrectly, the student does not have a chance to learn from those mistakes and improve on subsequent assignments.

In cases where assignments are sent one at a time upon completion, students have to wait as long as several weeks to receive grades and feedback, especially when assignments are sent back and forth via postal mail.

One student I know took a course that required students to send assignments via postal mail to the university. A designated department assistant forwarded the assignments via postal mail to the professor, who happened to live across the country. Grades and feedback were returned to the student the same way. The entire process, for just one assignment, took about a month.

This type of online learning can be a legitimate choice; however, students should always find out how assignments and grades are sent between student and professor and how long this process will take. Correspondence courses have been around a very long time, and there are still opportunities for this type of learning. I have taken about ten courses like this and enjoyed the flexibility of completing courses quickly or slowly, depending on my personal and professional schedule at the time.

Synchronous Courses

Synchronous courses are those in which students and professor are all online at the same time, usually in a chat room, and the professor teaches in real time on the computer. Most synchronous learning is still conducted via text (typing on the computer), but the trend is rapidly moving toward voice and even video chat on the computer. This makes learning in real time on the computer very similar to going to class. Students can hear, and sometimes see, the professor talk; view charts and graphics; and ask questions and participate in discussions with classmates during the class time.

Schools that have synchronous classes schedule them just as if students were going to campus for class. Students must read the assigned material and complete the written assignments prior to class. The only difference is that students are sitting at home in front of the computer rather than sitting in a physical classroom with their classmates and professor.

Students are expected to attend online classes and professors are required to record attendance, just as in a campus class. A benefit of synchronous classes over campus classes is that if you miss class, the entire online meeting is available for you to view or listen to at a later time. But even though you don't miss lectures and explanations if you miss class, you do miss participating in discussions. It's not uncommon to see grades drop when students routinely miss online class sessions.

The scheduled real-time meetings online can be a disadvantage for some people in other ways. Synchronous class times may not suit students' work or family schedule. These meetings are always in the evening and can be early or late, depending on students' time zones. For example, a 9:00 p.m. meeting on the East Coast would be meeting at 6:00 p.m. on the West Coast.

Before signing up for a synchronous online class, you should find out the online class schedules, the requirements for attendance, and the penalties for missing class.

Asynchronous Online Learning

Asynchronous learning is by far the most popular and most widely used form of online learning. In asynchronous classes, students have weekly start and end dates, during which time they must complete specific assignments and discussions. There are many different ways that professors structure asynchronous classes, and this can differ even within the same school. You should always find out how a school sets up this type of online class.

The typical structure is a weekly format with discussion and writing assignments due each week. The advantage of asynchronous learning is that as long as students complete assignments by the weekly due dates, they can do the work whenever it suits them within that time frame.

Just think, you'll never have to miss a family dinner with your kids because you have to be in class. You won't have to tell your boss you can't stay late at work to finish a project that is due the next day because you have to attend class. And the best part is that you will not have to miss out on another vacation opportunity because you have to attend class. Wherever you are, whatever is going on in your life at any given time, you can schedule your course work around everything else you have to do. I even know one instructor who conducted the first week of his class from the hospital.

"I'VE HEARD THAT ONLINE LEARNING ISN'T FOR EVERYONE"

Some experts say that online learning is not for everyone. Personally, I don't believe this is true. I think anyone can be successful in online classes as long as you have a commitment to spend the required time, the motivation to do well in the course, and the willingness to develop the learning habits outlined in this book.

We all know people who say that they need to be in a physical classroom with classmates and the professor in order to do well. Some people say that they need the external direction and procrastination-detector inherent in going to class with other students.

This simply means that it is more difficult to look the professor in the eye and admit that you did not do your homework or to convince your professor that you have a good excuse for missing the last class or the next one or whatever the case may be. These are excuses, and the problem with this way of thinking is that it doesn't work in online classes nor does it work in campus classes.

I have taught college classes both on campus and online and students aren't much different. The truth is, students who are not willing to do the work are not going to do any better in a class with the professor staring them in the face than they will in an online class. Either you are willing to work hard or you're not. Either you are going to make time in your schedule to do the class work or you're not. No professor, on campus or online, is going to do that for you.

The fact is that no one can make you successful if you don't want to do it for yourself. And if that is the case, then you can sink or swim just the same in an online class as in a campus class. Here's the good news, though—you don't have to sink at all. Anyone can learn to be self-directed rather than being accountable to a professor, parent, spouse, or whomever.

LEARNING STYLES

There are all kinds of excuses for failing or dropping out of online classes. Some experts say that learning styles have a huge effect on the level of success students experience in online classes. This is true only in cases where students do not know or understand their learning styles. The key to overcoming a specific weakness is to develop skills in other areas and thus create a balance across all the styles. Whether you are a visual, auditory, tactile, kinesthetic, global, or analytical learner, you can learn basic skills in all those areas to help you succeed in making good grades in online classes.

Visual learners read and write well, so obviously they do well in online classes. Auditory learners benefit from audio and PowerPoint lectures. Kinesthetic and tactile learners benefit from typing and being able to get up and move around whenever they need to do so. Everyone has more than one learning style, and although you may have a preference for one over the others, you can strengthen your weaker learning styles for more effective learning. Your preferred learning style, whatever that may be, can work for you rather than against you in the online classroom.

Some students are holistic learners and others are sequential learners. Holistic learners look at the big picture and wait to delve into the details. Sequential learners prefer to look at the details and then put together the big picture. There are a lot of resources online to help you determine your learning strengths and understand why some class activities are easier than others for you to complete.

ASYNCHRONOUS ONLINE CLASS STRUCTURE

This book is about how to succeed in asynchronous online classes. Correspondence courses need no further explanation or instructions. Synchronous courses have specific requirements for students to meet online at specific times with the professors and other students, just like going to a class on campus. If you choose this type of online learning, you will need to go through the college orientation and learn about the technology needed for your class.

Since most students take asynchronous online classes, they are the focus of this book. In these online classes, each week begins on a specific day and ends seven days later. Generally the last day of the week is the final due date for all weekly assignments, although there may be due dates as well during the week for some assignments. Most schools begin the week on Monday and end the week on Sunday, which means that all work must be submitted no later than midnight on Sunday each week.

Some schools begin on other days of the week. For example, one school where I teach begins each week on Wednesday, with all weekly assignments due no later than Tuesday of the following week. One of my friends teaches at a school where each week begins on Thursday and the final weekly due date is Wednesday the next week. I have also heard of schools that begin each week on Friday, and the final due date is Thursday the next week.

There are advantages and disadvantages to each type of weekly schedule and most students have little or no difficulty adjusting to whichever schedule is used at their school. If your school has Sunday due dates, then you will need to figure out if weekends are a good time for you to do a lot of your class work. Some students find that Saturday and Sunday are good days to carve out a huge chunk of time for completing writing assignments. Other students find that evenings during the week are the best time to work on class assignments because weekends are when they spend a lot of time with their kids and families.

Whichever is the case, you will have to consider all this when choosing a school and working out your weekly schedule. Students need to schedule at least some time every day of the week, but the amount of time each day can vary quite a bit from one individual to the next.

HOW TO BE SUCCESSFUL

The truth of the matter is that the majority of students who fail or drop out of online classes do so because they are not prepared to be independent, self-directed learners. These are just fancy words that mean some students don't know how to study, write, manage time, and organize weekly class work effectively. Developing and using these skills addresses all the learning styles so that students become stronger learners as their skills become more balanced across all the learning styles. This book addresses all of these topics in a logical, step-by-step process so that any student can experience success in online classes.

NOTES

2

CAN I DO THIS?

AM I SMART ENOUGH?

If you are still reading this book, then you are smart enough. And it's not really about "smarts" as much as it is about commitment, motivation, time management, and organization. If you are motivated and committed to making the time to study and complete class work every week, then I can teach you about time management and organization.

If you can read and type, then you can do well in an online class. During the first online class, successful students establish specialized learning skills and habits that will ensure success in all future classes. It's up to the student; the grades earned are directly related to the time spent each week in the online class.

Spending time does not mean that students are sitting in front of the computer for hours and hours every day. In actuality, students may only be on the computer a few hours a week. The time commitment involves reading, taking notes, preparing for discussions, and completing written homework assignments. Sounds a lot like "regular" school, doesn't it?

HOW MUCH TIME?

Some schools will specify how much time students should expect to spend every week, and others will not provide a specific time commitment. Students must be able to commit a significant amount of time per week to reading, writing, studying, communicating, and completing homework. This is not an insignificant undertaking, and one of the main reasons that students fail or drop out is simply that they are not prepared for the amount of time they need to spend each week.

Students who don't schedule their online learning time often end up procrastinating and find that the last day of the week has rolled around and they have not even completed the first requirement for the week. Being prepared and planning your time accordingly can ensure that this does not happen to you.

The general rule for a typical sixteen-week undergraduate course is three times the number of credit hours per week. This means that students need to spend a minimum of nine hours a week for a three-credit sixteen-week course. For a three-credit ten- or eleven-week course, students need to add three hours per week.

The big challenge is when students take a seven- or eight-week (half-semester) course. A lot of students think that taking half-semester courses means they can finish their degree in a shorter number of months. This may be true; however, students need to take into consideration the increased number of hours each week needed to complete a half-semester or a five- or six-week (accelerated) course. To do well in an accelerated course, students need to spend around eighteen to twenty-one hours a week.

Graduate courses require an even greater time commitment, with the general rule being four hours of work for every credit hour in a sixteen-week course. Most online graduate courses are approximately eight weeks, so that means a three-credit graduate course over eight weeks could require an average of fifteen to twenty or more hours per week.

Several other issues need to be taken into consideration when determining the number of hours you can expect to spend each week.

Table 2.1. Study Time for Three Credit-Hour Course

16 Weeks (Semester)	10–11 Weeks (Quarter)	7–8 Weeks (Half-Semester)	5–6 Weeks (Accelerated)
9–12 hours/week	12–15 hours/week	15–18 hours/week	18–21 hours/week

- Experience (The first online class always takes more time, because everything is new.)
- Reading comprehension
- Keyboarding skills

The time commitment is significant if you want to earn As and Bs in online classes. If you are satisfied with Cs, then you can get by with less time. Some people think they can get by with spending fewer hours and still make good grades. Students make their own choices about how much time they are willing to spend on their education. More time means better grades.

Before signing up for any online class, find out how long the classes run and then think very carefully about your daily and weekly schedule to figure out if you have the time. If you're not willing to find the necessary time each week, then you should put this book back on the shelf and don't waste your money. However, if you're committed to making As in your classes, then I invite you to continue reading so you can find out exactly how to do that.

SETTING PRIORITIES

The busiest people seem to be able to find the most time for whatever they need and want to do. Everyone has the same number of hours in a day. Most people need approximately eight hours of sleep, although they can get by with fewer hours on occasion when necessary. So when factoring in sleep time and working a full-time job for eight hours a day plus approximately one hour of travel time, most people are left with a grand total of approximately seven hours every day. In those seven hours, we all must fit in everything else we need and want to do.

When you decide to continue your education, you should devote at least one or two hours each day during the week to class work. On the weekends (or other days off from work), you should plan to spend another five to eight hours, and sometimes more if a big paper or final exam is due. Sheer procrastination can sneak up on students and they end up completing assignments in a rush, with just an hour or two left before the due date deadline. None of these situations is conducive to making As or Bs in an online class.

The very first thing all online students must do is examine their lifestyles, determine where and when education is going to fit, and then give some serious thought to setting priorities. Most online students have very busy lives that include work, family, and recreational time. However, everyone has time in each day that is unscheduled.

Not many people can honestly say that they never sit down to watch TV, surf the Internet, play video games or Wii, walk around the mall, shop, go to the gym, or any number of other activities. Everyone has time during the day or week that is not scheduled for work or family obligations. The problem most people have is giving up, albeit temporarily, nonessential activities in order to find time for school work.

The first thing you should do is simply write down what you do every day, including when and for how long. Start with whatever time you get up in the morning and go hour by hour. Once you've done that for a whole week, you may be very surprised to find quite a few free hours during the week that are spent on nonessential activities.

The most important task is to decide where education fits in your priority list. If you are a parent of young children or teenagers, or a caregiver of elderly parents or perhaps grandchildren, then family will be your first priority. If you also work, then your work obligations will be next, and education will come third. If you do not have family obligations, then work will be higher on the priority list, with education coming after that. You may be in a position where you can put education at the top of your priority list if you are a full-time student.

Whatever your personal situation, figure out where education falls on your priority list and then make sure it stays there. Too often, online class work is pushed aside in the day-to-day routine and all of a sudden, the week has gone by. Homework has piled up, participation never happened, and students are overwhelmed with catching up in two days on the work they should have been doing over the previous five days.

Spend some time reflecting on the importance of education in your life and realize that you will need to make some sacrifices in terms of recreational time and, sometimes, even sleep time. Students who routinely put online class work on the back burner when something else comes up that they would rather do, end up failing or dropping out of class. Success depends on dedication to placing and keeping education high on the list of priorities for however long it takes to complete a course or get a degree.

FINDING AND SCHEDULING TIME

Making good grades in classes is not about how smart you are or how hard you work, but about how smart you work. Keeping a schedule of tasks and due dates, by day and by week, will ensure that you have enough time to accomplish all the necessary tasks and to submit all assignments on time.

Successful online students say that scheduling class work and managing time efficiently are the keys to making good grades. Once you have access to the course, your first task should be to spend a couple of hours setting up your schedule of readings and assignments. This is the most crucial step in preparing for your online class. Students who skip this step may find themselves falling behind as a result of forgetting assignments or running out of time at the end of the week.

Before enrolling in a class, look through your calendar for the next two or three months. Mark your work responsibilities and tasks on your calendar. Do you have to travel for work? If so, when and for how long? Will you have access to the Internet at your hotel? (It is very rare these days *not* to have Internet access at hotels.) Do you have a laptop? If not, then taking an online class when travel is required at work is not a good idea.

Look closely at family obligations for about two months after a scheduled class start date. If there is a family reunion or big family birthday or a wedding or graduation or kids' sports events coming up, then you will need to figure out how much time will be involved in those events. All online professors will tell you that they have taken and taught classes when such events were taking place and they still managed to find a few hours to be online to accomplish necessary tasks. And because most online professors have also been online students, they don't have much sympathy for students who are unwilling to schedule class work around such events.

In cases such as these, there are basically three choices. First, schedule extra hours for school work in the weeks before the event so that you can finish your work early. Second, turn in your work late, take a huge grade reduction, and lose the good impression your professor has had of you up to this point. Third, wait to take the class later when there is not so much going on.

The first option is the best one, obviously—the second option not so much. This can also put students so far behind that they never seem to catch up. The third option can often completely derail a student's plans for an education because it is just too easy to keep finding reasons to put off enrolling in an online class. Some students never start down the path to their educational degree simply because they keep putting off taking that first class. Learn to schedule time and plan ahead. Always go for the first and best choice.

CALENDARS

Students who really want to earn As in their online classes have more success using two calendars and a "to do" list. One calendar is

---

Box 2.1. Finding Time for Schoolwork

I work long hours at my job and I just can't go to campus to take classes. At first it was hard to find time to get my schoolwork done at home and I missed a few assignments. Once I sat down and made a list of everything I do every day at home, I found one or two hours every day that I was wasting on things I did not need to do. So now I use those hours to do my online schoolwork. Working on my studying and assignments a little bit every day works for me, and I have not missed a single assignment in the past two semesters.

—New online student

---

for the length of the class (eight weeks, ten weeks, etc.). The other calendar is weekly. The "to do" list is daily. With all we do every day of our lives, if work for your online class is not scheduled monthly, weekly, and daily, something will be forgotten.

During the first week of class, enter all of the assignment due dates for weekly discussions, projects, and papers. Once this has been completed, then you can backfill your calendar with important dates for work and family obligations. If there are conflicts, now is the time to work these out on your calendar.

Recently I got an email from one of my students explaining that she had completely forgotten about the previous week's writing assignment and wanted to know if she could make it up. Since I provide a calendar of assignments and due dates in all my classes, I declined the request to make up the work.

Online students make choices to succeed or not succeed. If you want to make an A in your class, you must keep a list of tasks that need to be completed each day and make use of every free minute to work on those tasks.

Take some time now, before continuing with reading the book, to set up a system for your calendar, weekly tasks, and daily "to do" lists. Find out where you have time each day that you can use for class work.

Box 2.2. Don't Let This Happen to You

Dear Professor,

I'm sorry I didn't turn in my work last week. To be honest, I forgot I had signed up for an online class and no one called or emailed to remind me. Can I make up the work? I'll to do better this week.
Thanks,
Your Online Student

Dear Online Student,

Thank you for writing to let me know about your missing assignment. Unfortunately the late policy specifies that work can be made up only in case of emergencies. I look forward to receiving your assignments on time in future weeks. You may find it helpful to print the assignment calendar provided in the course and keep it near your study space so you don't forget due dates on weekly assignments. If I can answer any questions about the assignments, please be sure to let me know.
Thank you,
Your Professor

SELF-EVALUATION

1. How many credits is my class?
2. How many weeks is my class?
3. How much time do I need to spend each week on schoolwork?
4. How much time do I need to spend each day on schoolwork?
5. Are my reading skills average, above average, or below average?
6. Are my keyboarding skills average, above average, or below average?
7. What are my daily priorities?
8. What are my weekly priorities?
9. Where does time for reading and studying fit with my other priorities?
10. What can I give up to make time for reading and studying (e.g., television, social media like Facebook or Twitter, video games)?

CHAPTER 2

DAILY SCHEDULE

Write out your schedule for each day of the week. Add and highlight study times for each day of the week.

WEEKLY AND MONTHLY SCHEDULE

Write out your daily schedule for a week and a month. Add the study times from your daily schedule.

NOTES

3

WHAT DO I DO FIRST?

STEPS TO GETTING ORGANIZED

Now that your calendar is set up, it's time to set up a study space, gather materials, learn about the technology needed, and set up your email. These are first steps toward beginning an online class. After all this is completed, you will be ready to take the next steps to contact the school and, eventually, go into the online class. But first, you need to decide where you will study.

STUDY SPACE

Setting up a place to study and work on online class assignments can help you keep education high on the priority list. When you take the time to plan and set up a space that is your very own and that you use only for studying, you are telling yourself and your family and friends that education is a top priority.

A study space is a specific place where you can focus on class without interruption. Students who do this find that when they enter the study space, their mindset changes immediately to class work and it is easier to let go of distracting thoughts of other daily obligations.

Whether you are setting up an entire room or just a table in the corner of a room, set out your class materials so they are ready whenever you sit down to work or study, whether it's for fifteen minutes, several hours, or all night. Leaving class materials out for easy access will help you focus and stay organized. Organization is one of the primary factors in success or failure of online students. Organization starts with a specific study space.

A study space is as individual as the person who uses it. Some people need quiet and solitude, and others need music or the TV playing. A study space should have a way to close off the area from the noise of the rest of the house. This serves two purposes. First, you can be assured of quiet time so you can really focus on class during the time you are occupying the study space. Second, and perhaps even more important, you can organize your class materials and leave everything out for the next time you need to work on your class. A study space should be free of clutter and well organized with books, notebooks, computer, pens and highlighters, and whatever else you will need for your class.

Setting aside an entire room is not realistic in many homes. Another alternative is to create a study space in a room that is not often used, such as a guest room or a corner in a basement. I know some people who set up a quiet study space in a garage. You will need the ability to heat and cool the study space; in a garage or basement, this is most easily accomplished with a ceramic heater and a freestanding air-conditioning unit.

If the only place you can use for a study space is a corner of the family room or the kitchen table, this can work if you can be assured of a set amount of time each day that you can work undisturbed. Working on class assignments and reading and studying does not usually progress very well if you're in the family room with the TV going and kids playing.

If you are serious about continuing your education and getting a degree, then you have to be serious about your study time and space. This means that family and friends should respect your study time and space. Some people find that posting a study schedule and using a message board are good ways to help family members remember that they need uninterrupted time to prepare successfully for their class each day. You can post a short message on the door of your study space that says something along the lines of "I am writing my paper until 8:00 tonight." This lets family members know that what you're doing is important and that you will be available again at a specific time.

If noise is a distraction, try using a fan or a sound machine that blocks out noise from outside the space. Some students use ear protectors, such as those used when operating lawn equipment. Simple swimmers' ear plugs also block out distracting noise.

A study bag can provide a portable study space. If you need to study in different places, perhaps at work or at kids' ballgames, a study bag with laptop, textbooks, notebooks, and pens is a good way to keep class materials with you at all times.

ESSENTIAL MATERIALS AND EQUIPMENT

Obviously, online learning requires a computer and Internet access. Some people go to a public or local college library to get online; however, most students who rely on outside computer access don't do well in their classes. The problem is that they are tied to someone else's schedule—and they have to leave their house, just as if they were taking a course on campus.

Relying on a public-access computer is not going to work out very well when you want to write a paper late at night or take an online test at 5:00 a.m. This type of online access is fine for emergencies, but it's not good at all for everyday access to your online class.

Internet access is available through telephone connections and cable, as well as various wireless means. Check out what's available in your area and get Internet access in your home.

Other essential equipment includes a printer to make copies of all the lessons, class material, and assignments; printer paper; pens, paper clips, and stapler; hole punch; notebooks (large and small); doodle pads and Post-it notes; three-ring binders with tabbed organizers; and a large calendar.

You must have a way to back up and save all the work you do on the computer. Most people use a jump drive (also called a thumb drive) to store files in case of a computer crash. These little jump drives are available at places like Staples, Walmart, and Costco for very reasonable prices. These can now be purchased in bracelets, pens, and various other interesting trinkets.

The other option is to pay a yearly fee (usually around $50 a year) for a web-based backup service. I've used carbonite.com for several years. When I had to get a new computer, just a few clicks downloaded all my files to the new computer. Students find this service invaluable when their computer crashes and they cannot recover class assignments and files.

TECHNOLOGY

I have worked with students who knew more about technology than I did, as well as with students who did not know how to do much more than just turn on the computer. Every college that has online classes offers basic tutorials for students who need help with technology. All colleges have tech support that is available 24/7 for students and faculty who need technical assistance.

Take the time to read, study, and complete the technology tutorials available through your school. The tech support personnel can help you when you have questions about the online class. You should understand that professors are not technical experts and, while we can help with some questions, your best bet is to memorize the school's tech support toll-free number and never hesitate to call for assistance. Basic Internet and computer proficiency includes

- using MS Word to create and send files
- saving and naming files in RTF format
- using email

Knowing the basics will get you through the first class, and you will learn more as you use the computer for more tasks throughout your classes. The primary tasks will involve MS Word for writing and the Internet for researching. Most schools require that students use MS Word, so if you don't have that on your computer, you will need to get it. A free and compatible alternative to MS Word is OpenOffice.org.

Make use of all the knowledge and experience you have available through family, friends, local libraries, and community colleges. Free or low-cost basic technology classes are offered in some places; check for these in your area. Don't forget to check for technology resources and assistance through your online school. Schools want students to succeed, and they know that mastering the technology is a major element in every student's success.

SCHOOL EMAIL ACCOUNTS

If the school provides students with a school email address, then that is the only email students may use for all school correspondence. All school and class communications will go to school email. This includes registration and financial information, as well as all contacts from your professor and classmates. It is surprising how many online students forget to check their school email account. Until you develop this habit, you may find it helpful to include "Check school email" on calendars and daily "to do" lists. Get in the habit of checking school email immediately after turning on the computer every day.

PERSONAL EMAIL ACCOUNTS

If the school does not provide students with an email account, then you will have to provide your own. Most people have used email before they register for classes, and they tend to use for school whatever email address they have, such as thesmithfamily@aol.com or debbieandmark@yahoo.com. I've had students use email addresses such as onehotchick@yahoo.com or justcallmehoney@aol.com. Then there are those email addresses that are a bit, shall we say, racy. None of those are professional or academic email addresses, and they should never be used for school.

All students need to have an email address that includes their first and last names. Free email is available from Yahoo and Gmail. Create a special email account just for school that includes only your first and last names. Sometimes you may need to add numbers to your email address if someone already has an email address with the same name. For example, sarasmith may be taken already, so you can use sarasmith001 or sarasmith100. Some students like to use their names and the school name. Some examples would be sarasmith.allencollege (with a dot separating your name from the name of the college) or sarasmith_allencollege (with an underscore separating the names).

An email address with your name and school has three advantages. First, your school email is separate from other family members' email. I've had students who used a family email account and discovered that their children had unintentionally deleted important emails sent from the school. Second, this email address clearly identifies who you are when you need to communicate with your professors (and believe me, they will appreciate this). When I get an email from ilovecats, I have no idea which student is sending that email. In addition, such email names may be flagged by the email system as spam.

Third and most important, this email address presents a professional impression to classmates and professors. Eventually you may use this email address to send job applications and resumés. A professional email address presents a good first impression to prospective employers.

ACCESS TO SCHOOL INFORMATION

You have your computer, study space, and materials, and you have made a commitment to put your education near the top of your priority list. Now it is time to sign up and start preparing for your online class.

The first order of business is to learn your way around the online learning environment set up by your school. Most schools have specific websites for online students that typically include advising and registrar contact information, tech support, online classroom technology information, a bookstore, and a general orientation to online learning. Many schools also include information about accessing the online library, and some schools provide email addresses for students.

Students should write down, or print from the website, all important contact phone numbers and email addresses and file these in a notebook for easy access offline. Often, the time when you need these numbers is the time when you cannot log in to your online class. Always keep all contact phone numbers written down near the computer so you can find the information even when you cannot get online.

ACCESS TO CLASS INFORMATION

Although online classes begin on a scheduled day, students should never wait until that day to begin preparing for class. Some schools allow students to access the class from one to four days early for the purpose of giving them ample time to prepare before the first day. Other schools do not allow students to access a course until the first day. If you have access early, read all the syllabus and course information and start on your first week's assignments. If you do not have access early, start reading your textbook.

Some schools open the entire course on the first day so that students have access to all the lessons and assignments for all the weeks included in the course term. Other schools only allow students access to one week at a time throughout the course term. Prior to signing up for a class, find out when you will have access to weekly information that includes reading, viewing videos, discussions, and writing assignments.

Time management is one of the most important elements that will make or break your success in any online course. When your access to course material is restricted to one week at a time, you cannot read material ahead of time, prepare discussions, or begin preparing for writing assignments. In these types of classes, you will have more difficulty scheduling and managing time for all the necessary tasks you must accomplish each week.

From my perspective as an online professor and an instructional designer, restricting access is poor practice and unnecessarily limits students' ability to be successful in online classes. So be sure to find out about this before signing up for any online class. You need to be able to have access to all the course materials and assignments for the entire course from the day the course opens.

WHAT'S NEXT?

Scheduling, time management, and organization are all essential elements of preparing for your first online class. Good study habits are vital to success in all classes, whether online or on campus. Once you have set up a study space, calendar, and time schedule, it is time to develop skills that will ensure good grades in online classes.

GETTING SET UP FOR SCHOOL

1. Choose the location for your study space (or potential locations if you have not yet decided where to place your study equipment and materials).
2. List items you already have to use in your study space.
3. List items you would like to add to your study space.
4. List items that are absolute necessities in your study space.
5. Set up a personal email account that includes your full name. You will use this for all school-related communication (unless the school provides emails for students).
6. Write down all your school and class information below for easy access, in case you lose your Internet connection at some point during your online class.

NOTES

4

STUDY HABITS
J. Michael Tighe Jr., RN

HOW TO AVOID PROCRASTINATION

Good study habits are the key to successful completion of an online class. Procrastination is an easy trap to fall into when taking any class. Online students find that procrastination creeps up on them even more because there is no class to attend. Leaving study tasks undone causes a lot of frustration when students have to struggle to catch up and meet deadlines.

You will need to establish a study schedule that leaves a buffer zone in the event of an unforeseen emergency or illness. It's easier to stay caught up on schoolwork and even work ahead than to catch up once you get behind in the class assignments.

Reading and writing take up more time in an online class than in a regular class on campus. Reading takes more time than listening, and writing takes more time and thought than talking. Students who have difficulty reading can take comprehension or speed-reading courses to help brush up on their skills. Short writing courses are also available for students who need help with writing skills. As with any skill, reading and writing get easier and more effective with practice.

The best place to find help with reading or writing is through your college. All colleges now have online writing centers that offer proofreading services and even tutoring, free of charge, for students taking on-campus or online classes. Take advantage of these opportunities to ensure that your writing is the best it can be.

PLANNING COURSE WORK

The review and planning process should begin with your first access to the online class. You need to become familiar with the classroom by looking at all the buttons and tabs, and methodically clicking on each one. This is when your printer gets a workout. Print every page of information so you can make notes on the pages as you read them, and file each page of information in a class notebook. Highlighting assignments and due dates on the course calendar and course information documents will help you with budgeting time and meeting deadlines.

Take time on the first day to get out a calendar and write in the assignment due dates. Once you've placed all the due dates on the calendar, block out study time for reading texts and articles, watching videos, writing compositions, and composing discussions. Go ahead and estimate how much time will be required for each of the bigger papers and projects, like research, reading, writing, and editing—and don't be stingy with scheduling. It's better to overestimate than to underestimate the time you will need to successfully complete an assignment. Always take into account your reading and comprehension skills as well as your typing speed, because these will directly affect the amount of time you need for each assignment.

Once you have estimated the overall time requirements, break up this time into hourly and daily chunks and write it on the calendar. Include at least one hour every day or two hours every other day. For assignments that will take longer than a week, begin scheduling reading and research time several weeks in advance.

Do not let more than one day go by without doing something related to your online course requirements. Skipping a day promotes laziness and an attitude of "Oh well, I can do it tomorrow," and it's just too easy to slide into skipping several days. Then all of a sudden, you're behind in your work and it's very hard to catch up. Make time in your schedule to study every day and stick to it.

SAMPLE WEEKLY TIMELINE FOR STUDYING

Different schools have different start and end days for the course weekly work. Some start on Monday and end on Sunday, while others might start on Wednesday and end the following Tuesday. Take careful note of these timelines, as you will need to plan your work around them. Table 4.1 is a sample study schedule for classes that begin on Monday and end on Sunday.

The study and work process continues all week, every week, throughout the online course. The key is to plan to work some every day on class assignments so that you keep up and, hopefully, also stay ahead a bit. Whenever you have extra time, step up the hours spent on class work and get some future assignments at least outlined, if not completely finished. This could be an essential success factor if an emergency occurs at some point during the class that might require you to be absent for some period of time.

KEYBOARDING SKILLS

In an on-campus class, discussions take place via talking. In an online class, discussions take place via your keyboard. Think about this: Typing takes more time than talking. So this means that you will spend a lot of time typing on your keyboard during an online class.

Keyboarding skills are essential to successful online learning. All work is submitted in written format. Slow keyboarding skills can add many hours each week to class work time. Students who type faster will spend fewer hours than those who type slowly. There are online programs for learning to touch type and for learning keyboarding skills. Taking one of these short courses would be of great benefit in managing your class work time.

Table 4.1.   Sample Study Schedule

Saturday and Sunday	1. Finish assignments that have Sunday due dates. Participate in the class discussion (read new messages, respond to classmates). 2. Work on any ongoing group projects. 3. Plan to get a head start on the next week by reading, viewing videos, taking notes, and developing assignment outlines. 4. The goal is to have all reading done before the week starts on Monday.
Monday	1. Begin drafting weekly discussion or writing assignments that are due on Wednesday. 2. Check the discussion to see if there are any new messages to read.
Tuesday	1. Edit and proofread the discussion assignment that is due on Wednesday and post early. 2. If there are ongoing group projects, work on these. 3. Review all assignment due dates and instructions and notes. 4. Add notes where needed. 5. Create an assignment checklist from instructions. 6. Log in to the discussion; read all new messages; make notes and type up at least one response to a classmate's message; proofread and post in the discussion.
Wednesday	1. Begin outline for writing assignment that is due on Sunday. 2. Log in to the discussion; read all new messages; make notes and type up at least one response to a classmate's message; proofread and post in the discussion. 3. Check in with group if group projects are ongoing.
Thursday	1. Work on writing assignment that is due on Sunday. 2. Log in to the discussion; read new messages, respond to two more classmates; reply to any responses you have received. 3. Work on any ongoing group projects, including checking on group discussions. 4. Begin the next week's reading, viewing videos, etc., and start note taking.
Friday	1. Complete draft of writing assignment. 2. Work on any ongoing group projects. 3. Log in to the discussion; read new messages, respond to at least two more classmates; reply to any responses you have received. 4. Continue with next week's reading and note taking.

Slow typing does not mean you cannot or should not take an online class. Typing speed increases with practice and you will be getting lots of practice during an online class. Until your speed increases, however, be sure to allot plenty of extra time for typing discussions and written work. This extra time will decrease as you become more proficient with keyboarding.

READING

Reading assignments ensure that discussion work and writing assignments are clear and rich in content. You will be graded on how well you demonstrate understanding of the content. You will be expected to complete several different types of reading tasks in online courses.

Orientation is usually available and sometimes mandated by the school. Do not blow it off. This orientation is your overview to not only the online classroom, but to the entire college or university. You will find information about whom to call if you have technical issues, whom to call if you have problems with your online classroom, where to go to access library resources, how to get help with writing, and even such simple tasks as how to log on to the system and how to change your password.

The course syllabus contains information about specific assignments that are due throughout the duration of the course, the course calendar, and school and class policies and procedures. The announcements and questions forum is where you'll find important school and course notices. These may be changes in dates or assignments, or clarifications on course work. Content reading assignments may include the textbook, journal or research articles, or online webpages.

Here are some quick reading tips for better comprehension:

- Always read the introduction, conclusion, and summary in any text assignments first. This gives an overview of what to expect when you sit down to read the entire content in depth.

- Read all of the key words and their definitions, as these bring understanding to your reading.
- As you read the chapters in your text, try to identify key points in each paragraph. These key points will assist you as you write about your learning later.
- Journal articles and research articles generally have an abstract and/or introduction, along with a conclusion and/or summary of findings; read these sections first.

NOTE TAKING AND OUTLINING

For some reason, many students think that taking notes is done only when listening to lectures in a classroom. Note taking is also a vital part of studying when reading material each week in an online class. Taking notes as you review resources will help when it's time to write assignments. Think of notes as an outline for what you will write later.

Good notes will also save time and aggravation later when it's time to write a paper or summarize learning. One of my online professors once suggested that rather than using the infamous highlighter, it's more effective to write in the margins of the textbook or print copy of research articles. Students who prefer typing and keeping everything as Word documents can use red or blue font to make notes on documents. Notations might include such comments as "This will be good for a topic in Week 2" or "This will provide a source of information for the big paper." Notes must be meaningful and serve to help in remembering the material.

Some classes require memorizing formulas or terms, and the best study method is good old-fashioned flash cards. Use the small index cards, 3 inches by 5 inches, because they fit better in a jacket pocket. Write the term or formula on one side, and the definition or meaning on the other side. Flash cards can be taken everywhere, and it's a fast way to get in some quick study time. Students are often surprised at how effective even five or ten minutes can be when reviewing flash cards. I've seen people waiting in grocery lines, sitting in doctors' waiting rooms, and even sitting in traffic jams reviewing flash cards for class.

Notes, whether in the margins of textbooks or journal articles or on flash cards, provide a quick reference for studying for exams and for writing weekly compositions or longer papers. Good notes take some effort and extra work upfront, but the payback when it is time to write or study is well worth the effort.

Developing an outline for each assignment allows you to use notes and ensures that you meet the assignment requirements. Outlining also helps you maintain focus while writing. Outlining should become a strategy you use for every assignment in the course.

FOLLOWING DIRECTIONS

Professors often think that this is universally understood by all students; however, that is not the case. Following directions properly

Table 4.2. Sample Assignments and Success Strategies

Assignment	Success strategies
After reading the required text, write a two-page, double-spaced paper that addresses each of the following points: • Define communication. • Discuss how communication impacts your daily life. • Give two examples of good communication. • Give two examples of bad communication. • Identify the difference between face-to-face and online communication. • Explain why you think online communication can lack emotion. • Use at least two references to the required readings and cite them properly in your paper; include a reference list at the end. • Submit this paper by 23:59 on Wednesday.	• Take notes during the reading • List the requirements so you can check them off as each is completed. • Outline each of the key points of the assignment, using the notes you made during your reading. • Be sure that you thoroughly understand each question asked, so that you will properly answer the question. • If you don't understand a question, ask for clarification. • Write the assignment using the outline and notes. • Proofread the assignment using the checklist to ensure that all requirements were addressed thoroughly. • Run spell check and grammar check.

or not can mean the difference between a good and a poor grade on an assignment. All too often students glance through directions and then begin writing without looking at the directions again. This is why it is so important to always list the requirements for every assignment and then outline your assignment before starting to write.

Does this all take time? Certainly! But remember that these simple steps can make the difference between an excellent, average, or poor assignment.

ORGANIZATION

You will need to prioritize your class work to avoid last-minute, rushed assignments that won't earn much more than a C grade, if even that. Organizational tools and strategies that contribute to success are

- Computer and Internet.
- Backup Internet access plan if you lose power at home. There is nothing worse than getting to the deadline for a project or paper, and having your computer crash or losing Internet access at home. Make a plan ahead of time of where you will go and how you will access the Internet if you lose home access.
- Make sure there is a system in place to back up all your work. Making backup copies of all of your files and documents is essential. I use Dell online backup service for $30 a year. Carbonite.com is another online backup service and costs about $50 a year. These types of services will save you hours of rework in the event that you lose data.
- Printer for making copies of all class materials and lessons, as well as calendars with due dates.
- Assorted office tools (hole punch, stapler, Post-it notes, pens, pencils, etc.).

NOTEBOOKS

Successful students organize and maintain a three-ring notebook for each class, with dividers for course information and for each week of the class. For example, a binder for an eight-week class would include nine dividers. The first is for the syllabus and any other important information (school technical contacts, instructor contacts, and peer contacts). The rest are for weekly material and assignment instructions. Print all of the requirements, like required reading, discussion requirements, and any other assignments for each week. This helps break down the bigger course requirements into smaller, more manageable chunks.

TIME MANAGEMENT

Time management is the key to staying organized. Time management and organization are essential if you want to stay on track and keep your head above water. Consistently completing course work in advance will minimize stress. Try to budget time so that you are always a few days ahead of assignment due dates. Doing so allows some flexibility in the event of illness or an emergency.

Successful time management and organization takes commitment but it is worth the effort, especially if you get the flu or break your arm skiing or have a family emergency!

Commitment, organization, and time management are your best allies in success. Good study habits require hard work and discipline, but in the end it is well worth it. Set goals, make a commitment to complete these goals, get organized, and plan plenty of time in order to study successfully.

CHAPTER 4

ORGANIZING COURSE WORK

1. Set up a three-ring notebook with a Course Information tab and tabs for each week of the course.
2. Print all course materials including the syllabus, additional files provided by your professor, and announcements.
3. If your professor has provided a course calendar, print that and highlight due dates for assignments.
4. If no course calendar is provided, print a blank calendar and fill in the due dates for assignments.
5. Estimate how much time you will need for each assignment and for weekly reading. Write that on your calendar beside the due dates, and then schedule that time during the week (and write it on the calendar for each day).
6. Develop an outline for the assigned reading for Week 1.
7. Add notes to the printed list of assigned reading for Week 1.
8. Make a list of the instructions/directions for each assignment for Week 1. Use this as a checklist when working on the assignments.
9. Back up all the work you do on the computer.

NOTES

5

COMMUNICATION
Sara Bender, MS

COMMUNICATION ONLINE VERSUS FACE-TO-FACE

In a regular classroom, the professor gives out the information during class. Professors lecture and students participate in class and group discussions. Most communication takes place via talking and listening. In an online class, most communication between students and professors takes place via text, although some classes also include recorded lectures or real-time chat sessions.

When communicating within the classroom, students need to be professional, knowledgeable, substantive, and respectful at all times.

ANNOUNCEMENTS

Important information is communicated to students from the professor via announcements that are posted in the online classroom. Announcements may include clarifications of course content, changes in due dates or assignments, or other schedule revisions. You should always look for new announcements every time you log in to the course.

Table 5.1.   Characteristics of Classroom Communication

Professional	Writing reflects competence and academic ability. Comments should be free of spelling errors, grammatical errors, and general formatting deficiencies. Such errors indicate a lackadaisical attitude and give a negative impression. Text-speak, IM-chatting, swearing, and the like are not appropriate for the college classroom environment.
Knowledgeable	Messages should be content driven and not personal in nature. Study and learn the content before writing discussion messages. Provide specific examples and back up all opinions with course readings and other research. Provide citations and references so that others may follow up on the information if they wish to do so.
Substantive	Responses to classmates' comments need to be more than "I agree" or "You're right." These types of comments communicate nothing of substance, take up space in the forum, and do not further the conversations. Comments in response to others should be formulated to encourage additional critical thinking and induce further class discussion. Create responses that are likely to stimulate further thought by challenging ideas.
Respectful	Always address others by the names they used in the introductions. Never address your professor by his or her first name, unless specifically invited to do so. Be polite, courteous, and mindful of others' feelings when writing in online classroom discussions. Comments should never be evaluative in nature, and students should never correct classmates (e.g., say that someone answered the wrong discussion question). It's fine to disagree; however, be polite and courteous just as in a regular classroom. The online classroom should be a safe place where people can express new ideas, question themselves and others, and expand their thinking.

CLASSROOM INTRODUCTIONS

The first activity in most online classes is completing personal introductions. This is the online equivalent of the first-day ice-breakers that students do in regular classroom settings. Typically, students write a few paragraphs introducing themselves to the rest of the class. This is an opportunity to learn about each other and to gain an appreciation for the varying perspectives among the class members.

Introductions are the first impressions your classmates and the professor will gain about everyone in the class. The initial introduction will set the stage for how others view individuals throughout the entire semester. You should take the time and effort to create a concise, accurate, and descriptive introduction. Poor first impressions are difficult to change later on.

For example, some students write several paragraphs about themselves that are well organized into separate sections for school, professional, and personal information. Other students write one or two lines that don't say much more than where they live and a general "Hello." Which student will create a better first impression for the professor and classmates?

The key to creating a positive first impression is a comprehensive, yet concise introduction that balances your academic and professional status along with your goals and some personal information. Some students are comfortable sharing information about their families, hobbies, and travels. Others are not. Share what you are comfortable with but do write more than just a few lines.

Box 5.1. Classroom Introduction

Hi, everyone from Tacoma, WA! I am enrolled in the Criminal Justice program at XYZ University and I'm taking this class as one of my CJ electives. I've always been interested in profiling and hope to eventually transfer to a federal agency and use these theories in my work. For right now, though, I'm a full-time admin assistant in the court clerk's office, and I also take three online classes every semester. I will be graduating with my bachelor's degree next May. My hobbies are gardening, cooking, hiking, and camping. I'm looking forward to this class and getting to know everyone.

This is an elective class for my sociology major. I live in Rochester, NY, and work in web development.

Personal information about families, kids and grandkids, pets, and hobbies helps people get to know one another. There is a line, however, that should not be crossed when it comes to sharing personal information on a public discussion forum. Although your professor and your classmates are eager to learn all about everyone in the class, no one wants to know the intricacies of problems someone may be experiencing with work, school, family, health, or relationships.

Students should never share anything online that they would not share with a new classmate in a regular class. Think about it this way: If you wouldn't stand up and tell about something personal in the front of a classroom of thirty classmates and your professor on the first day of class, then you definitely should not write it online either. As you work on composing your initial introduction, you may want to consider addressing the following items:

- Name
- State of residence
- Occupation
- Course of study
- Why you're taking this course specifically
- What you hope to learn from the course
- Any other information that uniquely defines your life (e.g., Girl Scout troop leader, soccer coach, mother of four, etc.)

Even though you will not likely be required to respond to each and every classmate, you should at least read what everyone in the class has written. This is how students communicate and get to know each other in the online classroom. Choose classmates with whom you have something in common and respond to their introductions.

Responses should be personalized, genuine, and substantive. Although saying "It's nice to meet you" to everyone may be polite, it does not add substance to the conversation. Further, in a class of thirty or more students, making a short response to everyone creates hundreds of messages that everyone has to read. Instead of making numerous short comments that don't say anything, focus

Box 5.2. Greeting Your Professor

Hi, Professor! It's nice to meet you. I've loved all of my classes so far. Your pictures on the travel page remind me of some of our vacations. Makes me miss those places—especially since school is in session.

Nice to meet you, Professor. It is wonderful that you share those computer skills for newbies. Computers can be very intimidating to use if one is a novice. Your site has some links I found very helpful. See you in cyberspace.

Thanks for the greeting, Professor. I enjoyed seeing the photos of some of your camping trips. Your dogs are really cute. We have two dogs and five cats (want one?).

your responses on commonalities and work toward establishing a good rapport with several people in the class.

It is fine to ask questions to find out more about classmates—just be sure to return later in the week to see if the person responded. If he or she did, take the time to acknowledge the response and to thank the person for his or her time. Similarly, take the time to respond to all those who comment to your introduction. Thank them for their replies and answer questions appropriately.

Take a few moments to greet the professor in a reply to his or her introduction. Try to write something other than just "Nice to meet you." Usually most students can find a commonality to include in a response or a question to ask relative to professional information the professor has shared.

COMMUNICATION IN DISCUSSIONS

There are discussions in online classes just as there are in on-campus classes; the difference is that online discussions are written rather than spoken. Some class discussions may contain literally hundreds of messages if there is a high enrollment in the course. You need to take the time to read all discussions every week. The best way to manage all this reading is to log in and read new messages every day of the week. Missing a day can sometimes mean that there are over a hundred new messages to read the next day. Once unread messages start piling up, most students will not bother to read them all.

At the very least, you should read the first message that each classmate writes. If the content is interesting, then you can also read all responses to that message. If the conversation is interesting, that's the time to enter the conversation with a response to any message in the conversation. Each student in the class brings a unique perspective, and failing to read all the discussion messages means that those perspectives do not contribute to your learning.

QUESTIONS

Most online classrooms have a special area set up for course questions related to assignments, instructions, due dates, readings, and course content. Use this forum for course-related questions and do not email the professor with general questions when everyone in the class would benefit from the answers.

If, however, you have questions about your grades, concerns about interactions with another student, or personal emergencies that could affect academic performance, address these with your instructor via email. Class discussion forums are neither private nor confidential, so be careful what you post in the online classroom for all to see.

If you have a question that is technical in nature, always contact the IT desk for assistance and not your professor. If your query pertains to the policies or procedures of the course, first review every document posted in the classroom in an effort to find your answer. Then post the question in the course question forum.

EMAIL

All communications should be professional in composition, content, and tone. Always proofread messages and address the professor with his or her appropriate title (Dr., Professor, Mr., Mrs.). Never address your professor by first name unless invited to do so at the beginning of the class session (and even in that case, it creates a more favorable impression if you show respect by using the proper title).

Email messages should be concise—no more than a few paragraphs. Indicate the purpose of the email in the first sentence. Be precise about the action you wish the professor to take. If you have a question about a grade, don't just write "I don't agree with this grade" or "Why did I get this grade?" Provide examples (from the discussions, readings, etc.) and explanations regarding the grade you think you should have earned.

Keep emails professional and appropriate; do not write about personal problems. Professors do not need to be put in the uncomfortable position of knowing every detail of any student's life. While it's okay to tell a professor that your child was in the emergency room all night or that you have had a death in the family, don't spend time writing all the details. A simple one- or two-line statement is ample.

Most professors do not read long emails that contain every little detail of a student's divorce, problems with a teenager, or personal health and medical issues. They skim for the purpose of the email (which is usually asking for a due date extension) and then write back with a few lines to the effect of "I'm sorry to hear about [whatever the problem is]" and either grant or decline a due date extension. Professors are not counselors and they have neither the time nor inclination to become embroiled in conversations via email about the details of students' personal problems.

The email in Box 5.3 is not an exaggeration. Professors get long, involved, and rambling emails on various personal issues all the time. This email would have been all right if the student had stopped writing after the first paragraph. That's all the professor needed to know.

Box 5.3.   Emails to Your Professor

Dear Professor,

I need to request a couple of extra days for my assignment this week. I have been extremely stressed out due to my boyfriend moving out of my apartment and cleaning out my bank account and taking my computer. I won't be able to get to campus to use the computers to do my work until next week.

I'm afraid to drive cause one of my best friends told me that my ex-boyfriend is watching my house. I haven't seen him but my friend says she saw him hanging around two days ago and then last night he was driving by my house. So I don't want to leave my house in case he's out there watching.

I'm not sure what to do about this. My other best friend says I should call the police, but my sister says they won't do anything so don't bother. Like I said, I haven't seen him hanging around but it can't hurt to be careful. I'll plan to drive to the campus Saturday morning when my friends can come over to my house and go with me.

I don't think my ex would do anything, but it's bothersome when someone says they've seen him watching my house. I'm hoping my sister will let me borrow her laptop until I can get mine back. I don't know if my ex will give me back my computer and I can't afford a new one so I'll have to go to campus for the rest of this quarter to get my work done for my online classes.

If you have any suggestions about what I should do about my online classes, please let me know. I'll email you again as soon as I can get to campus to a computer there.

Thanks,

Your online student

Remember to keep personal issues private. If you wouldn't stand up in a classroom and say something in front of thirty classmates and your professor, then you should not write it in an email, either.

It is not necessary or encouraged for students to make excuses for late or incomplete work. If an assignment is going to be late, email to let the professor know but do not make excuses and do not say "I know you don't accept late work but I wanted to do the assignment anyway as a learning experience." Can't you just see the eye-roll? Take responsibility and just say the assignment is late and apologize.

COMMUNICATION WITH CLASSMATES

Typically, online students need not communicate with one another outside of the classroom. Students should keep all class communication within the classroom in the context of discussion boards, group pages, or chat rooms. This allows everyone the protection of documented interactions.

In-class communication also provides the professor with the ability to monitor not only the quantity of interactions, but also the content. When students choose to interact with classmates via email, sometimes these communications may be forwarded, modified, or copied to be sent on to someone else. Again, nothing is private or confidential in email; thus, all communications must remain on task and professional. Always avoid personal and confidential communications with classmates.

PROFESSORS' COMMUNICATION TO STUDENTS

Just as there are expectations for students in an online classroom, there are also expectations for the professor. Online education requires both parties to work effectively together to ensure the students' success.

Guidelines for professors' activities within the online classroom vary by the college or university. Some colleges have specific guidelines indicating that faculty must respond to each student's first discussion message in the weekly forum or respond to an overall percentage of contributions each week. Other colleges may not specify such requirements at all.

Some schools may require that faculty be online and responsive to students a certain number of days per week, whereas other colleges may not. So the question becomes, What kind of communication should students expect from professors and how often should that communication occur? What should students do if communication is not forthcoming in a timely manner?

Students should expect meaningful and timely feedback on their work each week for discussions, quizzes, tests, and all written assignments. "Meaningful feedback" is sufficient explanations so that students understand grades on various assignments. This type of feedback could be in the form of written comments or a grading rubric (sort of like a checklist) that indicates the points earned for meeting various learning objectives for the assignment.

"Timely feedback" generally occurs within five to seven business days, not counting holidays or weekends. Most schools now require professors to answer questions and emails within forty-eight hours. Many schools require a twenty-four-hour turnaround on emails and questions. Some schools require professors to grade all work within seventy-two hours. Before complaining about how long it takes to get grades from the professor, check the policies and procedures for your school.

WHERE IS MY PROFESSOR?

Students should expect every online professor to be visible and to have a presence in the classroom. This does not mean that professors will post messages in the discussion every day or respond in the discussion to every student, every week. This does mean that students will see evidence that the professor is working in the class. This evidence may consist of discussion messages, announcements, grades and comments on papers or in the grade book, answers to questions in the course, and responses to emails.

Occasionally a professor may seem to just disappear. If you don't see your professor in the discussions for the whole week or if you send an email or ask a question and do not receive a response within a couple of days, you should politely address this concern with the professor by email or by phone. However, if your professor disappears for more than a week, you should call your academic adviser and let him or her know of the situation.

Effective and meaningful communication follows specific protocols, and students should always try to handle problems with the professor first. If that endeavor fails, then it's fine to go to the academic advising department and follow their suggestions for the next course of action.

CHAPTER 5

GETTING STARTED WITH COMMUNICATION
IN YOUR ONLINE CLASS

1. Set up school or personal email account and check it every day.
2. Read and print all announcements in the class for the first week.
3. Read the information about your professor.
4. Write an introduction to post in the course the first week.
5. Read all classmates' introductions. Choose several with whom you have something in common and write responses to those classmates.
6. Keep a list of questions that crop up when you are reading class material and working on assignments.
7. Post questions in the appropriate place in your online classroom.
8. Post a quick thank-you when your questions are answered.
9. Set up a template for sending emails to your professor. Include an appropriate subject line (course number, full name, topic of email) and greeting as well as closing signature. Be sure to use this template whenever you need to email your professor.

NOTES

6

ONLINE CLASSROOM STRUCTURE
J. Michael Tighe Jr., RN

COURSE MANAGEMENT SYSTEMS

Online classes are set up in a course management system (CMS). There are quite a few different course management systems, but while there are differences in appearance, most work basically the same way. You will be given a username and password to log in to the online classroom. These are the basic features in most online classrooms:

- Classroom homepage
- Announcements
- Syllabus
- Course and/or college information
- Faculty information
- Communication areas (may include discussion boards and email, perhaps private message feature within the classroom, sometimes a chat room or live classroom area)
- Grade book
- Weekly lessons, lecture materials, tests, assignments
- Course tools (may include dropbox for sending assignments to the professor, small group areas, and whatever else your professor makes available as needed throughout the class term)

- Resources (may include document sharing, webpages, articles, etc.)
- Orientation or student manual for the online classroom (Many online classes provide a short orientation for the technical aspects of the online classroom. In lieu of this, sometimes the syllabus will include directions to the college online class orientation.)

CLASSROOM HOMEPAGE

The homepage is the main screen of the course and contains clickable links for most areas of the classroom and the school. School information can include connections to the library, writing center, student services, tech support, textbook information, and academic calendar. Becoming familiar with the links saves time later when you need help with something or simply need to ask a question that is not specific to your course.

Course announcements are displayed on the homepage and students can also access email, the grade book, weekly assignments, and other resources. The homepage also includes information about the course, program, school, professor, and introduction and question discussion forums. Explore all the links on the class homepage.

SYLLABUS

The syllabus is the outline of objectives, learning resources, and assignments for your class. Print it, read it, and make notes. Highlight important information and dates. Transfer these to your calendar and weekly "to do" list of assignments.

Course materials, such as textbooks and supplemental readings, will be listed in the syllabus. Many courses require reading material in addition to the text, and you will need to get access to those readings early in the course.

Information about weekly lessons and evaluation of your work is also part of the syllabus. Grading criteria, policies on plagiarism, course format, and bibliography will be included as well. Print a copy of the syllabus and be sure to read it before the start of class and review it weekly throughout the class.

FACULTY INFORMATION

It is always nice to know a little something about the professor. Typically, professors include information about their qualifications, credentials, and career experience. Some professors provide detailed biographies and others do not. Office hours and contact information generally appear under this tab.

GRADING RUBRIC

A rubric is simply a chart that shows requirements, point distributions, and the criteria used to assess each assignment. The grading rubric defines assignments and requirements so that students know exactly what they need to do in order to achieve good grades.

Always print a copy of the grading rubric and refer to it before, during, and after writing your assignments. Creating an assignment checklist with the rubric and the specific assignment instructions is your key to successfully completing assignments that are worthy of top scores.

GRADE BOOK

Online students use the grade book to track their progress throughout the class. Professors record assignment scores and comments explaining the scores in the grade book. Always read those comments every week and do what the professor says in order to improve your assignment for the next week. Not much irritates professors more than students who ignore grading comments and thus do not put forth the effort to improve their work as they progress through the course.

Depending on how the professor sets up the grade book, usually there is a breakdown of the course grade by weekly assignments, with separate sections for other assignments like papers or group projects. Many professors include a column in the grade book that displays a "current grade" or "grade to date," which is the running total of the cumulative grade at any given week during the class. If there is not a "grade to date" column in the grade book, ask the professor to set this up so that you will know your cumulative grade at all times during the class.

QUESTIONS AND ANSWERS

Most online courses have a Q&A section. Some professors set up a main Q&A forum on the homepage that students use throughout the course. Other professors prefer to set up separate Q&A areas within each week's assignment or discussion area. Either way, always read all new questions and answers every time you log in to the classroom.

The Q&A is where students post questions for the professor, yet the entire class reaps the benefit of the answer. Many professors ask students to monitor the Q&A and to help each other by providing answers when they can. Questions posted to this forum are generally about assignments or learning resources. Questions about grades or questions of a personal nature should not be posted in the public Q&A forum but should be sent by email.

STUDENT LOUNGE

Just as in a traditional school building, the online classroom will have a place designated for students to lounge and chat about topics not related to the course content. Professors call these areas by different names, such as student lounge, class café, and other similar labels. The basic purpose is to provide a place for students to socialize, just as they would in a physical class on campus.

Sometimes first-week introductions are posted in the student lounge area. Sometimes professors set up a separate area for introductions, in which case the lounge is used for casual, social conversation. This is also an area to share personal information like being an expert skier, an avid reader, or a Patriots fan.

Some professors monitor the online lounge and some do not. If you plan to use the lounge area, remember that it is a public forum and nothing is private or confidential. Do not use this area to post personal information that you would not be comfortable saying while standing in front of a classroom full of thirty students and your professor. And never use this area to complain about the course, the assignments, grades, or the professor.

WEEKLY TABS

Whether the course is six, eight, ten, or sixteen weeks, all course work will be located in weekly tabs. Objectives, learning resources, discussions, assignments, and additional papers or project work all fall under these weekly tabs.

DISCUSSION BOARDS

Discussions online are similar to discussions in a traditional classroom, except the conversations are in writing. Students share learning with one another by writing their thoughts on a given question, topic, or issue as assigned by the professor. Another element of discussions is commenting on other classmates' messages. Discussions can follow several different formats, so take some time to review how these are organized in order to best keep track of individual conversations.

Discussion expectations always include professionalism and courtesy toward classmates and the professor. Good grammar and

Table 6.1. Discussion Terminology

Term	Definition
Post or posting (noun)	The initial message written in answer to the discussion question, issue, or topic assigned for the week.
Post or posting (verb)	To enter a message into the discussion forum.
Responses	Messages written in reply to another person's message in the discussion forum.
Discussion board	The area of the course where the discussion forums are set up.
Discussion forum	A single discussion topic.
Discussion thread	A single conversation within a forum. There will be many threads in any given forum.

correct punctuation are critical in good writing. Always complete your writing in a word processing software program, run spell and grammar checks, and then completely proofread the material at least twice before posting it on the discussion forum.

Sometimes the terms used for various elements of the discussion assignments vary between schools. Some of the terminology may be used interchangeably. In order to understand the requirements and criteria, it is important that you understand the terminology used to describe the different elements of online discussions.

WEEKLY LECTURES AND STUDY MATERIAL

Online lectures come in several forms. Each week learning resources will be assigned to guide you through the content and learning objectives. This material can be presented in any of several formats:

- DVD
- PowerPoint

- Audio
- Video
- Real-time chat (called "live" or "synchronous" when two or more people are present in the course at the same time and are typing in real-time conversation)
- Webcasts (similar to videos)

These online presentations of course material offer the expert opinions and scholarship of the professor and other scholars in the course content areas.

DROPBOX

The dropbox is where students submit or upload assignments, papers, or group projects directly to the professor. Classmates cannot view anyone's dropbox except their own. Typically, the professor will make comments on assignments and return these with grades to the dropbox. Students can access comments through the dropbox area where the original assignment was sent to the professor or through the grade book.

DOC SHARING

The doc sharing area is where professors and students may upload files to share with others in the class. This is different from the dropbox, which keeps files private between student and professor. Doc sharing is a public course area that all students can access to download and save files.

Examples of documents that might be uploaded to doc sharing include specific information about the learning program, guidelines for writing and submitting papers, and documents or articles of interest submitted by colleagues or professionals. Sharing is of a professional nature and relevant to the current learning. This is not a place to share personal files or photos.

GROUP SPACE

Some classes require group projects or papers, and students need a place to work privately in their groups. The group space is like a mini online course and has many of the same components as the online class. The difference is that only group members can access the group space. There may be weekly discussion forums, chat rooms, file sharing, and email access.

WEB RESOURCES

Most online courses include web resources. These resources provide students with excellent references related to the course content area. You should save these resources in a favorites link on your browser so they will be available even after the class has ended.

OTHER COMPONENTS

There may be other components in online classes, such as message areas, journals, blogs, wikis, and other new technologies that are available to enhance students' learning experiences. If you find something with which you are unfamiliar, check back to the orientation materials or student manual to see if it's covered there. If it's not, contact your professor to ask for assistance. Always do this at least a week in advance of when you need to use a technological feature for an assignment.

NOTES

7

LEARNING ACTIVITIES AND ASSIGNMENTS

TYPES OF CLASS WORK

Online classes generally involve the same type of class work that can be found in on-campus classes. Tests, discussions, reports, presentations, and group projects are all examples of the kinds of assignments students are expected to do in both online and on-campus classes.

With the huge growth in technology over the last decade, many on-campus and online classes now also include assignments that involve working with technology. Examples of these would be blogs, wikis, podcasts, and audio or webcam presentations. Some classes have live chat sessions with classmates and the professor. These chat sessions involve either typing or talking and may be mandatory or voluntary.

All of these technology tools serve to make your learning experience richer. Visual learners will get more out of the content by watching a video or viewing a PowerPoint presentation. Auditory learners enjoy recordings of lectures.

The list of learning activities and assignments in this chapter is not all-inclusive. Innovative professors love to try new ways to involve students in the learning process. For example, some professors use Twitter or Facebook for class announcements. There's no end to the ways learning can be presented and assignments completed.

These are just a few types of activities and assignments that seem to be popping up in online classes more and more often.

BLOGS, WIKIS, AND JOURNALS

Blogs, wikis, and journals are the most common technology tools included in online classes. In all of these, students write about assigned content and then comment on other classmates' writing. These tools can be used for communication and collaboration among classmates or between students and professor. If one of these activities is included in your class, specific instructions will be provided for access and submitting your work. Here are some tips for working with blogs, wikis, and journals:

- Read the instructions carefully regarding both content and technology "how to."
- Create an assignment checklist and then outline the points you want to cover in your writing.
- Draft your comments in a Word document.
- Proofread and run spell check and grammar check before posting.

PRESENTATIONS (POWERPOINT)

Presentations in online classes generally are created in PowerPoint. If you do not have PowerPoint on your computer, you can create a Google presentation. This is a free program that, while not quite as feature-rich as PowerPoint, provides students with an alternative when presentations are required and PowerPoint is not available. The Google presentation program is accessed through Google Docs. Here are some tips for working with presentations:

- Read the assignment carefully and create a checklist of requirements.

- Outline the points you want to cover.
- Create a list of slides and organize the points on the slides.
- Go back to your slide list and rewrite the points in exactly the format you will use on the slides.
- Use bullet points and phrases (not sentences or paragraphs).
- Keep content to no more than six to eight lines on the slide.
- Make sure the text is large enough to read easily.
- Put one graphic or clip art on each slide, but not more than one.
- Be creative with the title page and conclusion page (more clip art or photos).
- Use a plain background on the slides; do not use patterned backgrounds that make reading the text difficult.
- Choose contrasting colors for the text and backgrounds.
- Do not use automatic timer slide transitions or sound effects.
- Do not use audio or video clips unless specifically asked to do so.
- Cite where you got the information and material for each slide, and include a reference slide at the end of the presentation.

INTERVIEWS

Interviewing provides students with additional information on class content topics. Interviewing usually involves composing questions and then recording answers. Sometimes students will be asked to talk to a person face-to-face and sometimes interview questions may be sent via email, with answers being returned to the student at a later date. Sometimes phone interviews are also used. These basic guidelines will help with successful interviewing:

- Always create a list of questions before an interview.
- Check the assignment to make sure your questions address the topics or issues required in the assignment.
- The list should have more questions than you think you'll need.

- Organize the questions for a smooth flow through the topics or issues.
- Take notes during the interview.
- Write the interview assignment as soon as the interview is over so that you get your first impressions and overall tone of the interview before you forget.
- Send a thank-you note to the interviewee, even if it's not required for the assignment.

GROUP WORK

Group projects are used in online classes just as they are in on-campus classes. Some students enjoy group work and others dislike it. Some people find that working in groups online is easier and others find it more difficult. A few basic guidelines can increase group productivity:

- Communicate often with your team members. Your professor will set up a discussion space for each group and you should monitor that area daily.
- Post ideas and questions and answers to teammates' postings daily.
- The group should elect a chairperson the first day. Then assign roles to each team member as needed for the project.
- Do your part and offer to help others.
- Do not miss a deadline; this will seriously tick off your teammates.
- Do not go MIA in the group discussion area; this will also seriously tick off your teammates.
- Do your part and do it on time.

TESTS, QUIZZES, AND LABS

Tests, quizzes, and labs are part of many online classes. Labs are used in science and technology classes and are set up differently for different types of classes. Your professor will explain in detail how to complete labs if these are required in the class.

Tests and quizzes are generally set up in the online classroom and students have access to these for one week. These may be objective assessments (multiple choice, true/false, etc.) that are automatically graded in the test area of the class. Other test formats might be fill-in-the-blank, short-answer, or essay questions; students type their answers into the test area of the class, and the professor grades the test later. Always read the syllabus carefully to find out what kinds of tests or labs are required in the class.

Sometimes colleges require one or more proctored tests during the term. This means that students take the test in the presence of another person. Proctors may be any school or library official. There are also testing centers in many cities where students may go to take proctored tests. Relatives and employers are not acceptable proctors for academic class tests. Check to see if a proctored test is required in the class and then make arrangements early in the semester to take the test according to the precise instructions given by the professor.

DISCUSSIONS

Learning does not take place in a vacuum. Interactive discussion brings forth sharing of students' prior knowledge and experience in such a manner that all students learn from each other. In most online classes, discussions are graded assignments and can count as much as 40–50 percent of the overall class grade. Just as in on-campus classes, online learning takes place through interactive discussion about class content.

Without interactive discussion, online students can feel isolated and alone. Discussions online provide opportunities for students to get to know each other and to share ideas and knowledge about the class content. In order to feel part of the class, you should always participate at least every other day in the discussions, even if the requirements are for fewer days.

You are responsible to prepare for discussions by reading and studying the class material. Read the discussion assignment carefully and make a checklist for each discussion that includes the content to be covered and the days and times when you will participate in the discussion. Then stick to your schedule.

Students don't always understand how to write for discussions. Most students are used to writing essays, answering written discussion questions, writing opinions in journals or on tests or for homework, and writing research papers. Writing for discussions is a bit different.

Discussions are more informal. This does not mean you should post work that has misspellings or grammatical errors or is unorganized and off-topic. Discussions are reflective, exploratory, and constructive, and this is where you share ideas with classmates. Just like in a spoken conversation, students state opinions, ask questions, and argue points. And just like in a spoken conversation, students need to take the time to go back to read what others have written and then respond to those messages. The goals for online discussions include the following:

- Thinking critically and creatively
- Reflecting on what others say
- Backing up statements with facts and documentation
- Assimilating the information
- Applying knowledge to relevant issues

The best way to successfully complete discussions is to participate often. Engaging in meaningful sharing of ideas and knowledge will help everyone learn the course content. Frequent and meaningful participation shows the professor your leadership skills as well as your interest and motivation to do well in the course. A few basic strategies can ensure that your discussion work is of the highest quality possible:

- Review the discussion requirements.
- Read the class material.
- Take notes on the reading that relate to the discussion topic.

- Write out the initial discussion entry addressing the discussion topic or question. Use your notes. Organize in a coherent manner. Stay on topic.
- Proofread, spell check, and grammar check your work.
- Make your posting on time. If you can post a day or two early, that is better and will make a good impression on your professor.
- Respond to classmates' postings. Respond more than the minimum requirements. If the requirement is for two responses, then make three or four responses.
- It's okay to disagree; do so politely and supply facts to back up your comments.
- If you agree, that's fine, too. But write more than just "I agree." Explain *why* you agree and write at least five to seven sentences (more is better).
- Read the responses you receive. Answer those responses.
- If the professor posts information or questions, respond to at least one or two of those.
- Participate at least three days each week; every other day is best.

This may sound like a lot of work, but consider this: You can type messages any time of the day or night and save them on the computer until you are ready to go the discussion board and post the messages. When reading classmates' messages, you should immediately type and post a reply while the information and response ideas are fresh in your mind. It is a lot like listening to someone make a comment in a regular classroom and then saying something back. The only difference is that students read what people say and then write a message back instead of listening and talking.

Discussion requirements vary among different schools. Some require students to post messages three, four, or five days every week. Others have no requirements in regard to how many days or how many messages students must post each week. Know what the requirements are in your class and schedule this time on your calendar.

PREPARING FOR CLASS WORK

The primary means by which students can earn top grades is preparing properly for completing class work. There is a process involved in successfully completing class assignments:

- Read the assignment.
- Create a checklist.
- Read class material.
- Take notes.
- Create an outline.
- Write a draft.
- Proofread, organize, and rewrite.

You should use this process with every assignment; never just write an assignment and then turn it in the same day. This means, of course, that you can't procrastinate. Always do the work early and don't wait until the last minute and then rush through the assignments. Using effective study skills can ensure that you develop good habits starting the first week of your online class.

LEARNING ACTIVITIES

1. Make a list of the different types of learning activities required in your online class.
2. Put a star beside any activities with which you have no prior experience.
3. Read the instructions carefully and make a list of questions that you need answered about any specific activity.
4. Print the instructions and make a checklist for each learning activity. Include this in your notebook in the appropriate week.
5. If there is a group project, add the weekly tasks to your calendar and highlight due dates each week. Schedule weekly communication on several days each week and stick to that schedule.
6. Note days when discussion messages are due each week and add those to your calendar. Schedule participation for several days each week and stick to your schedule.
7. If you are required to use technology for some assignments (e.g., PowerPoint, blogs, wikis, etc.), get set up for those now, before the week the assignments are due.

NOTES

8

WRITING: RESEARCH AND PLAGIARISM

WRITING OVERVIEW

Writing can strike fear in the heart of even the most experienced writer. I don't think there is anyone who hasn't looked at a blank page and felt a sense of terror that they won't be able to think of anything to write. The good news is that anyone can learn to feel comfortable with writing. It's simply a matter of following a step-by-step process and writing a little bit at a time.

People write for many reasons: creative writing, scholarly writing, business and technical writing . . . the list goes on forever. People learn how to write at a very young age and continue to write all through school. Many people find that writing is essential in their jobs and careers. Everyone communicates in writing in some manner or another.

Communicating effectively in writing is a series of skills that can be learned. Some of these skills include grammar, sentence structure, spelling, choosing the most effective words to convey meaning, and proofreading to ensure the quality of the intended message. These skills are used every day in online classes for every type of learning activity or assignment.

Students need to have good writing skills to make top grades in online classes. All colleges have writing centers that provide individual help if students need additional assistance in academic writing. Most colleges now also provide free tutoring services for all students, on campus and online. Students need to make use of these resources if the first writing assignment comes back with a low grade and comments that indicate the writing needs improvement.

If this happens to you, don't give up. But don't wait to get in touch with the school writing center. If you do this immediately and arrange for tutoring, it's possible you can still make an A or B in your online class. If you wait to get help with your writing, you won't make a good grade in your class and you'll just postpone the problem and have to deal with it later.

Students who don't make the time to improve their writing skills will eventually fail a class or end up dropping out of school. Everything you do in an online class is submitted in writing. Don't wait to get help with improving your writing skills.

PLAGIARISM: WHAT IT IS AND HOW TO AVOID IT

Plagiarism and cheating are serious offenses at all schools. Cheating generally involves more than one student. For example, taking an online test and then giving the questions and answers to a classmate is cheating. Another example would be giving a paper you wrote for a class to a friend to use in another class. Cheating also includes purchasing an essay or paper online and submitting it as your own work.

Plagiarism generally involves one student who copies information from a source (e.g., a book, a news article, or a webpage) for an assignment and then submits that as his or her own work. There is intentional plagiarism and unintentional plagiarism. Even if it's unintentional, the consequences are the same as for intentionally plagiarizing someone else's work.

The best way to avoid suspicion of cheating or plagiarism is to know what these mean and how to avoid them. Generally and simply, plagiarism is using someone else's thoughts or words without giving credit to the original author or creator.

Intentional plagiarism needs no explanation. Copying material from a source for the purpose of using it as one's own work is blatant plagiarism. This is wrong—it is a copyright violation and a very serious academic honesty offense.

Unintentional plagiarism happens when students do not understand how to conduct research and cite sources properly. All too often, students copy words directly or paraphrase without citing the original source. While ignorance can result in unintentional plagiarism, it is still a copyright violation and a very serious academic honesty offense.

Cheating and plagiarism have become big problems in colleges. Most professors now scrutinize all students' papers for plagiarism. All colleges use plagiarism-detector programs and professors have the ability to very quickly scan every paper written by every student. Some schools require students to use these programs to scan their own papers and then provide the scan report with their paper when the assignment is submitted for a grade.

RESEARCH

Except for opinion papers or reflections of learning, all other papers involve researching information to include in the paper to back up your own opinion, analysis, evaluation, and conclusion about a topic. Research is not as difficult as it sounds. The first part of research is locating information.

Locating Information

All schools have online libraries that students can access with their class login username and password. Students will then be able to access news and journal articles for material on the topic of the assignment.

Locating credible, accurate, and reliable sources of material and information is easy if you know how to search for information. The first step is searching for information specific to the topic. Researching for topics and information is sort of like playing the game "Free Association," where someone says a word and another person says the first thing that pops into his or her head.

This is what happens when you research information for a topic you need to write about for an assignment. Start with a general topic and see what turns up. You'll get more ideas from looking through the first list. Then run a search on a new idea and you'll get more ideas from looking through that list.

After choosing the general topic, identify several subtopics. Finally, narrow the focus of your paper to one issue within one of the subtopics. This can be done in a step-by-step process. Here is an example using the topic "online high schools" as a guide to narrowing the focus of any topic or issue:

1. Start with a general search on your favorite search engine or the online library databases at your school. Your professor will tell you if you can use Internet sites or whether you need to limit your research to the library.
2. Type in the general topic and scan through two or three pages of hits (don't click on any of those yet) and see what subtopics are available.
3. In searching for information about online high schools, you see the term "virtual high school" several times. So change the search terms to those words.
4. Run another search, and again scan through the pages and see if anything is interesting or relevant.
5. Next, look for articles and webpages on other topics related to virtual high schools. One article stands out: It's about using gaming in virtual high school classes.
6. Now it's time to narrow the focus and run a new search on virtual high school class games.
7. Then you find some articles about how virtual high schools are using video game learning activities in online courses. That's a good topic for a writing assignment in the area of online high schools.

Evaluating Validity, Accuracy, and Credibility

Some professors allow students to use Internet search engines such as Google, Bing, or Dogpile. If you are allowed to use Internet sources in your work, be very careful in evaluating online information for credibility, accuracy, and reliability.

- Look for the author of the article or webpage. A credible author will have education and work experience in the field and will most likely provide email contact information. There should be some evidence that he or she has written extensively on the topic.
- Check the publication date. The general rule is that anything more than five years old is not acceptable. Some professors specify no sources older than two years. Check the requirements for your class.
- The material should be supported with facts and details that can be verified in other sources.
- The school online library will have people to help you locate and evaluate articles and websites for use in writing academic papers.

Using the Material and Information

Once you have located several articles or webpages to use for the assignment, it's time to read, highlight, take notes, and outline the source material for the assignment. Outline the assignment with the topic of the paper and several points to cover. Use the assignment instructions as a checklist to make sure all requirements are included.

After going through relevant sources, choose three to five sources with material to use in the assignment. Read each article thoroughly. Complete the outline as you gather information. Add or omit points in the outline as you begin to get a better idea of what you want to write about. Highlight relevant information in each source that you may want to quote or paraphrase to support the points in the paper, and take notes from these highlighted areas. Sometimes it's helpful to note on the outline which articles or sources you plan to use for each section of the paper.

Now that your research is completed, it's time to start writing a draft of the paper. Plan to write at least two drafts and a final copy. The next chapter covers how to write a paper.

GETTING SET UP FOR WRITING

1. Find out the style your professor requires for documentation of sources (e.g., APA style, MLA style, etc.).
2. Locate the formatting information provided by your professor. Print and study that information. Use it when you are writing.
3. Ask questions whenever you don't understand how to cite sources in your work.
4. Look up your school's academic integrity policy. Print it, study it, and know how to avoid trouble.
5. Learn how to use your school's online library services. Contact the librarian if you need help.

NOTES

9

WRITING PAPERS

Students have to write papers in every online class. Even math, computer, and science classes require written papers. You will find several types of writing assignments in online classes, such as reports, essays, reflection, and other short papers of around five or fewer pages. There are also longer research papers, which are typically between five and fifteen pages in undergraduate courses and up to twenty-five pages or more in graduate courses. These types of writing assignments are common in all subject areas.

Following a systematic process for writing papers can help ensure the successful completion of these types of writing assignments, not to mention decreasing the stress most students feel when faced with writing an academic paper.

GETTING ORGANIZED

You will need to approach your writing assignments in an organized and methodical manner. Preparing for writing assignments makes completing them much easier. The most important issue with writing papers is to begin early and plan for at least five days to complete a writing assignment.

In the previous chapter, you learned how to conduct research and prepare notes with citations and references for the paper. Now it's time to begin writing. Here are some writing tips to help you complete your writing assignments in an efficient and effective manner.

BRAINSTORMING

Begin by listing the assignment instructions. If a topic has been assigned, make a quick list of everything you can think of pertaining to that topic. If you have to choose your own topic, write a list of topics that you would find interesting to write about. When you have chosen a topic, make a list of everything you can think of about that topic. Keep this list so you can add to it as you begin researching and reading about the topic. During the research process, you may decide to change the topic, depending on what you find while researching.

RESEARCHING AND TAKING NOTES

The next step is to begin researching, reading, and taking notes on the information you find. Work on this for a couple of days. If you find other related topics that you may want to use instead of the original idea, make another list with ideas for the new topic as you progress with your reading. Take notes during the research and reading process. These notes will help you formulate an outline for the paper.

THESIS STATEMENT

Now you have your topic and some information about the topic. Analyze the information and decide the purpose of the essay. For example, essays may be descriptive, instructive, argumentative, or explanatory. Essays may compare and contrast issues or topics. The assignment will most likely explain what type of essay is required.

Think about the purpose of the essay and then decide how the topic you chose will fit that type of essay. Then write one sentence that describes the purpose of the essay and the importance of the topic. This is called the thesis statement, and it will be included in the introduction of the essay.

Along with the thesis statement, you will need to list several important points about the topic. These will be the basis for the body paragraphs of the paper. At this point, you should list as many points as you can think of, or points that you have found in your research. Try to ensure that each point relates to the purpose of the essay. Add some notes to each point; these can be words, phrases, or complete sentences. Also note which resources support the ideas that are listed under each point.

OUTLINING

The outline is the basic organization of the essay. A lot of students skip this step in the essay process, and what generally happens is that the essay rambles and even goes off-topic. Use a simple outline with headings, points, and ideas and examine the finished outline carefully to see if the points are all necessary and have a logical flow.

FIRST DRAFT

Once you have completed detailing the outline, you can begin writing. At this point it is important to remember that this is just the "idea" phase of writing a paper. Spelling, grammar, punctuation, and so forth do not matter at this point because this is a rough draft. All you need to worry about is just getting your ideas and thoughts on paper.

Box 9.1.   Sample Outline

I.   Introduction
   A.   Thesis statement
      1.   Purpose
      2.   Importance of topic
   B.   Background
   C.   Summary of points
II.   Body paragraphs
   A.   First point
      1   Supporting information, ideas, words, phrases
   B.   Second point
      1.   Supporting information, ideas, words, phrases
   C.   Add as many more points as you need for the essay.
III.   Conclusion
   A.   Restate the thesis.
   B.   Summarize the important points.
   C.   State the conclusion.
IV.   Reference list
   A.   Sources for material used in the essay.

When your first draft of ideas is completed, then it is time to go back and add headings to the paper. This is where the outlining and researching you have already completed comes in handy. Take the headings directly from the outline and insert these in the paper in the appropriate sections. Next, review the notes and material from your sources and place those in the paper in appropriate paragraphs to support what you have written in the draft.

SECOND DRAFT

Put the first draft away for a day and then read it again. Clarify points by adding more details, explanations, examples, and related personal or professional experiences. Review the research notes and make additions to each section with relevant research material to support what you wrote. Review and rewrite the introduction and conclusion so that these two sections correlate with the thesis, validation of points, and conclusions you have made about the topic.

Read the entire paper from beginning to end to edit for organization of points, proper paragraphing, and a smooth flow of subtopics. Make sure the paper covers the points detailed in the introduction and that you have stayed on topic throughout the paper.

DOCUMENTING MATERIAL FROM SOURCES

- Go through the paper from beginning to end, one paragraph at a time, and check placement and accuracy of citations for material you've used from your sources. Use the proper manual (e.g., APA or MLA) for examples and models to ensure your style is correct.
- Add your reference list. (Copy/paste the sources you used when writing—remember when you formatted the references for each article?)
- Check the reference list for alphabetical order, punctuation, spacing before and after punctuation, parentheses, capital letters, italics, and so on. Again, use the proper manual (e.g., APA or MLA) for examples and models to ensure your style is correct.

PROOFREADING

- Read your paper aloud from the beginning to the end.
- Highlight areas to correct—don't stop to correct while reading aloud. At this first reading, you are looking for content, organization, and flow.
- Next, read your paper aloud backwards. Read the last paragraph, then the next-to-last, and so on. At this reading, you are

looking for writing errors. Mark (highlight) errors to correct, but don't stop your reading to fix them now.
- After reading your draft twice, correct the places you've highlighted.

Now the writing process is completed, and you have a polished paper to submit for a grade. This process can be used for everything you write throughout your college career. Plan to spend significant time on writing assignments and schedule the required time in your calendar.

PLANNING AND SCHEDULING ENOUGH TIME

Most students do not take the proper time to plan, brainstorm, outline, research, and write multiple drafts of papers assigned in their college classes. Students who do spend from nine to fifteen hours per week working on writing assignments will be far more successful than those students who spend four, five, or fewer hours.

For short papers, schedule at least one hour per day, for five days prior to the due date. For longer papers, schedule one hour per day for five days two weeks before the paper is due, and then schedule two hours per day for five of the seven days immediately prior to the due date.

Procrastination will cost you an A in the class. Procrastination can cost you a B or C as well. The fact is that students just cannot write a decent paper in one or two days. Professors know, beyond the shadow of a doubt, when students write assignments on the day before they're due, or on the due date.

WRITING YOUR FIRST ASSIGNMENT

1. *Start early.*
2. Estimate how much time you will need for each element of the assignment and write it on your calendar. Schedule time each day and stick to your schedule.
3. List the assignment instructions and check off each one as you complete it.
4. Brainstorm ideas, using an outline, list, or cluster/mind-mapping techniques.
5. Do your research and take notes. Keep all this in your notebook.
6. Write your thesis statement.
7. Make an outline.
8. Write the first draft.
9. Refer to the course information about properly documenting sources.
10. Proofread, revise, edit, and proofread again. Get a friend or family member to help proofread.
11. Review the proper format for saving and naming the assignment file.
12. Turn in the paper on time!

NOTES

10

COMMON MISTAKES TO AVOID

Thomas E. Escott, MSEd

IT HAPPENS TO EVERYONE SOONER OR LATER

Confused? Overwhelmed? Terrified? Panicky? These are a few of the emotions that first-time online students experience. Often students drop their first online course in the first week because everything is new and they can't seem to figure out anything. These are all normal feelings, and you need to make sure that you are prepared and do not become so overwhelmed that you want to drop the class or you miss assignment deadlines.

Here is an interesting fact that most students don't know: Even online professors and experienced online students have some degree of anxiety immediately prior to the start of an online course. It's just like when we were all in elementary, junior high, and high school, with the excitement and anxiety that naturally occurs at the beginning of any new semester or school year.

New students make several common mistakes, especially in the first weeks of their first online course. Learning how to avoid these will lead to a successful online experience.

MISTAKE 1: SKIPPING OUT ON NEW STUDENT ORIENTATION

Sometimes students are so anxious to get started in their course that they don't take the time to thoroughly go through the new student orientation that colleges offer. Some schools require completion of orientation prior to beginning class and some do not. Whichever the case, students need to give the orientation their undivided and focused attention from beginning to end. Make sure you understand everything and contact tech support (or whatever contact person is listed in the orientation) to answer any questions that may come up.

Students must know the school policies for online learners and how the course technology works. Missing this information in the orientation materials can, in some cases, lead to such frustration that students end up dropping out before the end of the first week of class.

MISTAKE 2: NOT CALLING TECH SUPPORT

First-time online students are usually eager to access their new course. When entering the web address of the course and their login information, sometimes they find that the website can't be found or the login information provided to them by the school does not work. This can be very frustrating and can cause immense anxiety and fear about not having time to read everything and get the first week's assignments completed. There are some specific steps to follow if you cannot log in to your course in Box 10.1.

So, finally, you're all set to begin the course. You are organized for the week and have been able to log on to your course. You find the first online reading assignment and click on the appropriate link. Then you wait . . . and wait . . . and wait. Your computer seems to be frozen and you start to panic.

There are several reasons why this might happen. In some cases, the problem may be with the course management system and will be resolved shortly. In other cases, it could be your computer. Mul-

Box 10.1. Technical Issues with Access to the Course

- Check to make sure that your computer meets all of the system requirements for the course and has the correct versions of required software.
- Find the email with the required information from the school admissions office. Check to make sure that you have entered the required information correctly.
- If you are still not able to access the course, contact the person who sent you the instructions or call the tech support number.

timedia, including videos and graphics, will stretch a computer's resources. If the computer or Internet connection is slow, call tech support to find out if they can help. If the school tech support cannot help, try calling your computer manufacturer tech support and your internet service provider (ISP) tech support.

I've had issues where school tech support said they couldn't find the problem and could not help and neither could the ISP tech support. But my computer manufacturer tech support team found and fixed the problem. Make the school's tech support your first call, not your last resort. Don't assume that technical issues will be resolved without intervention. And don't panic—there is always someone who can help resolve technical problems.

MISTAKE 3: NOT IDENTIFYING YOUR EMAILS

Students are expected to read and respond to all emails sent from the school and professor in a timely manner. When sending emails to the school or to the professor, always format the subject line with the course number, your full name, and the topic of the email message.

Some of the email subject lines that I have seen in student messages include: "HELP," "Question," "I'm lost," "Need help with course," "Emergency." I think you get the idea. Some professors state in the syllabus that they will not respond to unidentified emails. Box 10.2

Box 10.2. Email Protocol

- Identify yourself in the email subject line. Always include your course name and number, your full name, and one or two words regarding the topic of your email message.
- Check your spam folder daily before deleting those messages to make sure emails from your school or your professor are not being redirected into the spam folder.
- Set up folders in your email program for school information and for course information. Save all emails you receive from the school and your professor in the appropriate folders. Do not ever delete emails after reading them, because you might need to refer to them again at some point in the future.
- If you have been assigned a school email address, you must use that email address to communicate with the school and with your professor. Get into the habit of checking your school email every day.
- If your school does not provide a school email account, set up a separate email account through Gmail or Yahoo to use just for school. This email should have your full name before the @ sign.
- When you get an email from your professor, be sure to respond no later than midnight the following day. The same day is better.

illustrates some policies and procedures for sending and receiving emails that most schools and professors require of all students. Failure to follow these rules can mean frustration for you and for your professor.

MISTAKE 4: WAITING A WEEK TO LOG IN TO THE COURSE

If I had a dollar for every student who was enrolled and had proper and correct course access but did not log in until the end of the first week, I'd be a millionaire right now. At the same time, if I had to give back a dollar for each time I put something off until the last minute, I would be broke. It's so easy to procrastinate!

In order to increase the likelihood of succeeding in an online class, it is imperative that you log in to the class no later than the first day. Some schools allow access from one to four days prior to the official start date of the course term, and if that is the case, you should log in before the first day.

Accessing the class early can help in two ways. If a mistake is made in the login process, either by you or by the course administration, tech support can assist in correcting the problem without losing any valuable course time. If, however, you wait until the last minute to try to access the course and then you have technical or login issues, you are already behind and will need to work extra hard to catch up.

The other way this can help is that you can begin printing all the course information before the first day of class. Most students need at least a couple of days to read and digest all the course information and get organized before they begin on the first week's reading and assignments. If you wait until the first day of the first week, you only have seven days to get organized and do the work before the deadline. Taking a few extra days before the first day can have a significant and positive impact on your ability to do well on the first week's assignments.

MISTAKE 5: WAITING UNTIL MIDTERM TO GET THE TEXTBOOK

Each online course probably will have extra materials or textbooks that you need to purchase. This information is identified during the registration process. Order materials as soon as possible so that you don't miss any reading assignments. Not having the proper materials for the first week of class can put you behind right from the start. This can cause more work, a lot of frustration, and sometimes even panic. Professors have little patience when students' work is late because they didn't get the textbook in time.

When ordering books, double-check to make sure you have selected the correct edition and ask how long it will take to be delivered. If you have given yourself enough time, you won't need to request priority shipping. If delivery is after the course begins, then it's worth paying the extra shipping charge to get the materials shipped overnight. Then be sure not to make the same mistake next time.

MISTAKE 6: ASKING REDUNDANT QUESTIONS

Usually there will be a place in the course where you can post questions. Most professors request that all course-related questions be posted in the appropriate forum in the course. Before asking a question, review the syllabus, course information, calendar, and assignment instructions. If you still can't find the answer, ask.

MISTAKE 7: NOT FOLLOWING INSTRUCTIONS

Sometimes online learners begin reviewing instructions for an assignment and discover that they have no idea how to begin. Sometimes they don't understand the assignment requirements and sometimes they don't understand the related readings. Frequently the student will issue the cry "I'm totally lost!"

A preventive measure is to read the instructions carefully and make a checklist of all requirements prior to beginning the weekly readings. Review chapter 4 on study habits and follow those steps to ensure that you complete assignments correctly and thoroughly.

MISTAKE 8: NOT SUBMITTING ASSIGNMENTS PROPERLY

New online students are often nervous about submitting their first assignment. They want to do their best and are anxious about their first grade. Starting a course with a poor grade is so discouraging! There are different types of assignments, and each one may have different procedures for submission.

There may be discussion assignments posted on a discussion board, written assignments submitted directly to the professor through a dropbox, blogs and wikis, or assignments that will be developed using multimedia or other web-based tools. Don't be nervous! The first thing you should do if you're not sure how to submit an assignment is to review the new student orientation materials.

The orientation will include information about submitting each type of assignment. This information might also be found under on-line "Help" or in a message from your professor. Some courses also have a tutorial section or a student manual where you can look up information about submitting assignments. If you're still not sure, try tech support. Often they can walk you through the process. If all else fails, ask your professor.

MISTAKE 9: NOT SUBMITTING ASSIGNMENTS ON TIME

Each week, you will have several assignments. Some of the assignments will be due at the end of the week, while other assignments, such as discussions, may be due earlier in the week. To make sure that you submit assignments by the due dates, you need to review the calendar every week and create a daily "to do" list.

Remember to print this schedule and write in other appointments that you may have during the week so that you can plan ahead to complete all of the week's assignments on time. You will also avoid having your assignment marked late and losing points.

Another helpful strategy is to use an online calendar and/or a "to do" list that includes the capability of emailing you reminders of due dates. Gmail and Yahoo both have calendar features that send email reminders of events, appointments, and due dates.

MISTAKE 10: PARTICIPATING IN DISCUSSIONS
ONLY ONCE A WEEK

Students often ask if they will be interacting with other students in their online course. The answer is definitely yes! One way that students do this is through discussion assignments. After completing the readings for the week, students will be asked to write answers to specific questions or to reflect on the reading.

There is usually more to the assignment, however. You may be required to respond to one or more discussion messages from your classmates, adding additional value to the discussion. Often there are two due dates during the week for discussions, one for the answer to the question and the other for responses to classmates.

To receive full credit for the discussion assignment, make sure that you have reviewed the requirements for the assignment and understand what makes a good response. Sometimes examples of good responses are provided in the orientation materials, and the professor may provide discussion examples in the course information.

MISTAKE 11: NOT REVIEWING GRADES
AND COMMENTS ON ASSIGNMENTS

Professors are amazed at how many students never bother to look at their grades or read the comments on graded work. Professors spend a lot of time writing comments in order to help students improve their work; it is irritating, to say the least, when students' work does not improve. In fact, in some cases, students make the same mistakes over and over because they haven't read the professor's comments on their assignments.

Always read everything the professor writes about your work. Make notes and lists and then incorporate those improvements into your work the following week. The professor is there to teach, but if you don't do what we say, then we can't help it if your grades are lower than you'd like.

MISTAKE 12: FORGETTING TO RELAX,
READ, REVIEW, AND REFLECT

By now you shouldn't be feeling quite so overwhelmed as perhaps you were at first. The tips in this chapter can be summarized in two words: "Be prepared!" All of the information for your success has been made available to you. All you need to do is read and study the information, reflect on how you can use the information in this chapter, then review it again and file it where you can easily find it. Your success is in your own hands.

NOTES

11

WHAT KIND OF STUDENT DO YOU WANT TO BE?

PROFESSORS KNOW WHAT IT'S LIKE TO BE A BUSY STUDENT

Sometimes students expect sympathy from professors when life events get in the way of completing schoolwork. Making this assumption, however, can backfire, because professors have also been online students. In some instances, professors *are* online students, while also teaching and working a full-time "day" job.

Online professors continue their teaching through whatever life throws their way. Odds are that they did the same when they were online students, too. One professor I know had a baby three weeks into an eight-week class. She logged into the class five days that week, and her students never even knew she had a brand-new baby.

I know professors who have gone through chemotherapy while teaching online classes and never missed any time from the class. Other professors have maintained their teaching responsibilities while in the hospital following surgery or recovering from a severe illness.

I have taught online classes (and taken online classes) through surgeries, hurricanes, ice storms, and power outages that lasted more than ten days. My philosophy is that you figure out a way to do what you have to do. And there's always a way if what you have to do is important enough to find a solution.

Some students wonder how professors can do all that. But it's not just professors. I've had online students who have successfully completed classes during all kinds of unexpected events including having babies (well, those events are expected but not scheduled!), surgeries, family illnesses and emergencies, and natural disasters like hurricanes and blizzards.

It takes excellent time management skills, advance planning for emergencies, and perseverance to work through whatever comes your way. Successful students and professors find ways to get it all done. Sometimes people have to temporarily give up socializing and recreational activities. The key word is "temporarily," because nothing lasts forever, and motivated students can find ways to work through a week or two of rough times and still do what needs to be done for work, family, and school.

BEHAVIORS GUARANTEED TO GET ON YOUR PROFESSOR'S NERVES

Professors have been students and know all the excuses and stunts in the book. One student told me he was taking his wife on a surprise anniversary trip to the Cayman Islands, and it was so primitive there that they didn't even have Internet. He wanted to miss the first two weeks of class and make up the work when he got back.

Well, obviously I knew better, so I went online and found several hotels that had Internet cafés where he could do his work. I also looked up the cruise line and, sure enough, the ship had Internet access. So I wrote him back and told him that the work needed to be done on time. I provided him with the list of places where he could get online. The student dropped the class.

Why do these behaviors pluck at professors' nerves so much? Because professors know that these behaviors are a result of a poor attitude about learning.

Box 11.1   Behaviors Guaranteed to Get on Your Professor's Nerves

- Make excuses for late work.
- Miss the professor's online office hours (or online lecture).
- Don't read all the course material. (Your professor can check statistics in the course to see exactly what areas you clicked on and how long you were there.)
- Wait until the last day of the week to participate in discussions.
- Participate in the discussion on the first day of the week and don't return all week.
- Ask questions that are clearly answered in the syllabus or other course information.
- Call the professor by his or her first name.
- Email the whole class with complaints about the professor or the assignments.
- Correct other students or tell them what to do (or not to do).
- Ignore the professor's emails.
- Don't read assignment directions and instructions.
- Ask what your grade is instead of looking in the grade book.
- Ask what you have to do to bring up your grade in the class.
- Ask for extra credit assignments, especially in the last couple of weeks in the class when you have a failing grade.
- Ask the professor to look over your work before the due date.
- Ask if you can do an assignment over for a better grade.
- Plagiarize or cheat on assignments.
- Send file attachments that your professor cannot open.
- Treat your professor like your personal servant (e.g., "I have to talk to you right away. Call me at 000-000-0000 by 5 p.m. today").
- Argue like a rabid dog over grades.
- Threaten to "go to the dean about this."
- Send emails without greeting or signature and no name and class in the subject line.
- Try to get through the class without buying the textbook.

(continued)

> **Box 11.1** *(continued)*
>
> • Expect the professor to answer questions and emails immediately.
> • Send an email asking why you haven't gotten an answer to an email you sent an hour (or two or three) ago.
> • Use rude or inappropriate language in emails or discussions.
> • Tell the professor that a vacation trip is a "surprise" from or for someone or is a "once-in-a-lifetime vacation" and then ask for an extension on the due date.

DO YOU WANT TO BE STUDENT A OR STUDENT B?

Online professors get numerous emails from students who have excuses for turning in work late. This is a huge aggravation, and professors see this as evidence that students are not motivated and dedicated to their education. Certainly life events occur, and certainly there are times when unexpected catastrophes occur. The problem is when students use these as excuses for requesting due date extensions and other extra considerations that their classmates, who do their work on time, do not receive.

Planning Ahead for Vacation

Student A wrote the first week of class to explain that he was going to be away the sixth week of the class. Ordinarily, he said, that would not be a problem because he had a laptop so he could work while away from home. The problem was that this particular trip was an annual twenty-mile hike and camping trip in the mountains with his father and brother in a place where there was no cell phone service. He wanted to request permission to turn in the work for that week early. He was not leaving until the second day of the week and returning very late on the last day of the week and planned to participate in discussions on those days.

In the same class, Student B wrote the first week to explain that he was going to be away on business during the eighth week of class. He explained that he was going to be in training sessions all day and in the evening and would not have time to get online to do his schoolwork. He wanted to know what to do about his assignments and discussions that week.

Student B wanted me to tell him what to do about his planned absence. Class work is always the student's responsibility, and professors are not tasked with making schedules for students or managing their time. In the case of Student B's inquiry, my response was to put the responsibility where it belonged, with the student.

Student A wrote back immediately, saying he understood and appreciated the consideration. He did complete the work as planned and did not receive any zeros in the class. In fact, he completed the class with an A. Student B never wrote back, and he did not submit discussions or the paper that was due that week. He did finish the class but earned only a C−.

Box 11.2. Professor Responses to Request for Vacation Time

Dear Student A,

I appreciate your notifying me of your trip during class. You are most welcome to complete and submit the assigned paper for that week early. You do need to understand that the discussions cannot be posted early nor can you earn credit for posting discussions late (that would be like going to a classroom the week before or after a class and sitting there talking when no one is around). However, it sounds like you'll be able to fit in the required participation requirements.

Thank you for taking the time to plan ahead for this absence during Week 6 of the class.

Cordially,

Your Prof

(continued)

Box 11.2. (*continued*)

Dear Student B,

I appreciate your notifying me of your trip during the eighth week of class. Your options for submitting the work are the same as if you were taking this class on campus. You may turn in the written paper early or late, as you choose.

The discussions cannot be posted early nor can these be made up if not posted during the week they are assigned. That would be the same as going to your classroom on campus a week early or late and sitting there talking when no one is around.

My suggestion is to look at your travel and training schedule and figure out if there is some way to complete your work. Thank you for the advance notice of this business trip. I look forward to hearing from you regarding your proposed solution to this planned absence from class.

Cordially,

Your Prof

Requesting That the Professor Accept Late Work

Online professors receive numerous emails requesting acceptance of late work. Reasons for not completing work on time vary and, in some cases, students have legitimate emergencies. Most cases, however, involve a lack of effective time management. All too often students are caught up in unexpected overtime at work or in children's activities and just do not realize how much time these events take away from school study time.

Online students appear to request late work acceptance more often than do traditional campus students. It is a whole lot easier to send off an email with excuses for not completing work than to walk into class and admit, eyeball to eyeball with the professor, that you did not do your work. I have found that in a traditional campus course, students tend to stutter and stammer over their excuses for not doing homework. In online courses, students tend to write a page or more of details explaining their circumstances.

Box 11.3   Student Requests for Acceptance of Late Work

Dear Professor,
   I am writing to inform you that my work due in two days will be late. I have a family emergency that requires out-of-state travel. My mother-in-law fell and broke her hip and will need surgery immediately. We are leaving this evening and I'm not sure when I will return home. I have my laptop and will continue with my discussions, although some may be a bit late. I will also continue to work on the report due this weekend and turn that in as soon as possible, if not by the due date.
Thank you,
Student A

Dear Professor,
   I know I've been away from class for two weeks but I didn't have a computer. My girlfriend left and took all my electronic stuff, including my computer and TV and DVD player and X-Box 360 and all the games. I have been calling and trying to get back all my stuff. I finally called her parents and they said they would help but nothing so far. I still don't have a computer. I promise I'll make up all the discussions and homework for the past two weeks. I might not be able to do the work this week either unless she gives me back my stuff.
Thank you,
Student B

Professors tend to be sympathetic, for the most part; however, that does not mean a penalty-free acceptance of late work. Student B's email is about average as far as excuse emails go. In this case, Student B never showed up in class again. In cases of emergency, most professors will grant an extension for up to a week, or sometimes two, depending on the nature of the emergency. Always contact your professor immediately in cases of emergency. We are more than willing to help out by making arrangements for accepting work late if necessary. Keep your professor's email address and your academic adviser's phone number where family members can locate those contacts if necessary.

Student A and Student B

Student A does not make excuses for late work. In fact, Student A rarely, if ever, turns in work late. Student B, on the other hand, misses quite a few deadlines during the semester and always has an excuse. Do you want to be Student A or Student B?

NOTES

⑫

MAINTAINING MOMENTUM

YOU'RE IN THIS FOR THE LONG HAUL

You are now ready to begin your first online class; however, everything you've learned and accomplished so far is only the beginning. There is another important element in ensuring success and good grades in your educational endeavor. After the class begins and a few weeks have gone by, the problem for some students becomes sustaining the effort for the duration of the course.

MOTIVATION AND COMMITMENT

Good intentions, positive habits, or new behaviors cannot compensate for lack of motivation and commitment. The usual stresses of going to class on campus are not issues in online classes. Students don't have to worry about the commute, parking, traffic jams, nasty weather, and babysitting issues. There are no worries about being late to class, about family or personal illness, or set-in-stone schedules.

Instead, the stress is related to finding time and sticking to a daily schedule of completing schoolwork. Procrastination is a serious issue for all students, but more so for online students. The cause of failure in online classes is not related to inability to do the work but rather to the tendency toward procrastination.

Most students start out with good time management schedules and the commitment to do their schoolwork to the best of their ability. They are motivated to succeed. But sometimes life just gets in the way, and motivation takes a hit. All students need effective strategies to help maintain motivation and commitment when the going gets tough.

BALANCING RESPONSIBILITIES

Most students juggle school with other responsibilities for family and work. Most people also need time for sleep and recreational activities. The course calendar, weekly calendar, and daily list are strategies to help balance these responsibilities. Yet even with the best planning and time management strategies, unexpected events will occur from time to time that can throw even the most organized student off stride.

Students start out classes with the best intentions, and most of them manage to keep to the schedule for the first few weeks. Then an unexpected event takes precedence and the schedule is forgotten for a few days or even a few weeks. Then all of a sudden, students can be so far behind in assignments that catching up is an insurmountable obstacle.

The best way to handle these types of situations is to be prepared in advance. Family events like weddings, reunions, birthdays, and funerals can take up a lot of time in daily or weekly schedules, especially if travel is involved. Vacations must be planned around everyone's schedule, and sometimes this means taking vacation when your online class is in session. Parenting young children and teenagers or caring for ill and elderly family members places even more responsibility and stress on students, who need to find time to complete their schoolwork.

EMERGENCIES

When students miss class time and assignments because of emergencies, professors will most likely understand and grant due date extensions. If, however, a student does this more than once, the professor will not look kindly on the second request and may not grant extra time more than once. This can result in one or more zeros in the grade book that can bring down the overall course grade enough that an A or B for the class is simply not possible.

All professors have had students who seemed to have one emergency after another. One week the kids are sick. Another week the student is sick. Another week the power goes off during bad weather. Yet another week a distant family member is hospitalized and the student needs to travel out of town. Unbelievably, there's even another week when the student has to travel unexpectedly for work.

Some students have one excuse right after another for not getting assignments completed on time. Thankfully it is very rare for any one person to have this much bad luck during one class term. If you are unfortunate enough to have more than one emergency during a class, the best option might be to drop the class and start over again the next term. Unfortunately, many students who drop out do not return. If you are considering this option, make sure that there is no other choice but to leave school to deal with multiple family or personal emergencies.

Students who continually submit work late, for whatever reason, rarely earn good grades in their classes. When work is late or incomplete because it was written in a rush at the last minute, its poor quality will be reflected in poor grades.

PLANNING AHEAD

You should set aside several hours every week beyond what is needed for weekly assignments to work ahead and complete some future assignments early. Stay ahead in required reading. You can also type and save answers to discussion questions ahead of time. Always start working on writing assignments several weeks early, making notes and an outline, and perhaps even writing a draft of the paper.

Successful students stay organized and work ahead in their classes, filing completed work in folders (on their computer and hard copies in their notebook) for each week so they can submit the work when it's due. These students also participate in online classroom activities frequently, at least four or five days every week. Whatever the minimum participation requirement, successful students exceed that by at least two or three days every week.

PARTICIPATION

Frequent and substantive participation keeps students on a schedule, maintains interest, helps form friendships for professional and academic support, and demonstrates initiative and leadership. Professors do notice this and are impressed and appreciative of the interest and dedication.

If you demonstrate that you are putting forth every effort to learn and do well, your professor will be more inclined to help you out in any way possible should the need arise. If you participate in discussions five out of seven days every week, making several responses to classmates and encouraging further conversations, then when you need to miss a day occasionally, you will still have met the minimum requirements for the class and your grade will not suffer. If, however, you participate only enough to meet the minimum requirements and then you miss a day, your grade definitely will show the poor quality of the work.

PERSONAL SUPPORT SYSTEMS

Even the most successful students go through periods of time during their college education when they wonder if they'll be able to make it through. When the going gets rough, a strong support system can make the difference between success and failure—going missing or dropping out of the class. What is a support system and how can this help?

Support systems can be family, friends, classmates, and coworkers. Not every person has all these support systems. Some people have several support systems and some people have only one or maybe two. The best way to build a support system is to share your educational goals with the people who are important in your life.

Tell your family, friends, and coworkers about your classes. Tell them why going to school is important to you. Don't be afraid to talk about the lifestyle changes that you've had to make to accommodate your study time. Ask for advice when potential problems come up in your family life, at work, or with your schoolwork. Talk to friends and coworkers about what you're studying in class.

ACADEMIC SUPPORT SYSTEMS

In most online classes, students get to know each other pretty well during the course session. Students meet and greet each other during the introductory week and learn about each other's educational goals, professional and family lives, and personal interests or hobbies. The lounge or class café area provides a place for students to talk about topics and issues that are not related to the course content. Students can ask for advice and offer suggestions to classmates who might be experiencing problems in maintaining a balanced schedule.

Sometimes no one posts questions or comments in the lounge area, and sometimes students keep a running dialogue going throughout the session about family, work, current events, and other topics of interest. I like to encourage students to share pictures of themselves, their families, pets, vacations, kids' sports events, weddings, and so forth. This is a nice way to get to know classmates.

Often students will find good friends among their classmates and will keep in touch long after the class has ended. This is how people start an online professional network and support system. Keep in contact with classmates of similar interests, and you can share future class and work experiences after the course is over and everyone has gone their separate ways to new classes.

Professional networking provides another support system that can help students remain motivated and interested in their studies. Students should consider joining a professional networking website such as LinkedIn, where they can meet other professionals in the same field.

All of these support systems provide students with connections to other people who are taking classes, looking for a new job, or working in the same field. Connecting with people online gives students an avenue to ask for and offer advice on everything from studying and work to family and other responsibilities.

REWARD YOURSELF

Studying, working, parenting, caring for family members, volunteering for good causes, and even playing at fun activities all take time. There are only twenty-four hours in every day, and some of that time must be spent sleeping. Often students find that recreational activities have to go. Sometimes students find that sleep time has to go. All of this is so that students can find extra time to study and complete assignments for classes.

The payoff can be a short or long time in the future, depending on whether a student is just taking a few classes for a certificate program or starting from the beginning to earn a degree. Whichever the case, everyone should set up a reward system for successfully reaching goals.

Set up a reward that you can look forward to when the first class is over. This can be dinner out with family or friends or maybe even a weekend away at the beach. Plan something relaxing, whether for an evening, a day, or a weekend. Then, as each new class begins, plan something fun and relaxing to look forward to when the class is over.

Look ahead in your educational program and set up rewards for more long-term goals. Perhaps you might want to take a week's vacation when you reach the halfway mark and a cruise at the end of your program. Rewards are as individual as people, and you need to think about this carefully and choose something that is important to you. When the going gets tough, you can look forward to a reward for successfully accomplishing your goals. Always remember that each class completed is another step toward your final goal.

WHO IS YOUR PROFESSOR?

In all workplaces, there are excellent, good, not-so-good, and very poor bosses, managers, supervisors, and employees. The same holds true for the field of education. During your time in school, you will meet excellent, good, not-so-good, and very poor online professors. Likewise, professors meet excellent, good, not-so-good, and very poor online students. Students often wonder about online professors and what they do all day and all week while students are busy reading, studying, participating in discussions, and writing assignments.

Contrary to popular opinion, online professors are not faceless ogres, with only names on a computer screen, who wield the red pen searching for mistakes and inferior ideas, slashing and marking up students' work with relish.

I am not a faceless name on a computer screen and am definitely not an ogre. Not even close. I am your online professor, and I have taught thousands of students in both online and regular classrooms. I love my work, and I am very good at what I do. Most online professors are just like me.

All online professors genuinely and sincerely want their students to succeed. Success means that students have met the goals, learning objectives, and outcomes for the course. When students earn good grades, they have demonstrated mastery of these course goals.

We like to see students work hard, complete class work on time, and earn good grades, just as we did when we were in school. Our goal is for all students to learn the course information. Students cannot do this, though, unless they are interested, motivated, and willing to work hard to complete the class assignments.

NOTES

ADDITIONAL RESOURCES

Visit the Online Learning Guide blog (onlinelearningguide .blogspot.com) for up-to-date information about online learning.

ADD YOUR RESOURCES HERE

Use this space to write down school contacts, online learning tutorials, and other online resources you find before and during your online class.

ABOUT THE AUTHOR AND CONTRIBUTORS

We have been online students. We know, understand, and have experienced the excitement, anxiety, just plain weariness, and sometimes even second thoughts about going to school. So who are we, where have we been, and where are we going?

Leslie Bowman is a career educator whose experience includes teaching in elementary school and college, instructional design in Homeland Security and educational technology online programs, and training new online faculty. She currently works full-time teaching online undergraduate and graduate courses in English, writing, communications, educational technology, and criminal justice. Her published works include articles about distance learning, online teaching, technology, and school safety; a book about personal safety; and a historical novel. Leslie's advice: "Always strive to be a lifelong learner. I am a lifelong online learner because not only am I teaching online classes pretty much full-time, I am also taking online classes."

J. Michael Tighe Jr., RN, started on his first online learning journey in 2007, seeking a master of science in nursing degree. Although familiar with the Internet and computers at work as a registered nurse, he was not prepared for what was to come next in this new scholastic journey. Mike chose the online learning experience for the convenience of learning at home or on the road, rather than traveling to the traditional campus classroom. While in graduate school, Mike maintained a full-time (forty-hour-plus) position as a senior clinical analyst, a full-time graduate program, and still had time to enjoy his second passion in life beyond nursing—downhill skiing at Sugarloaf Mountain in Maine.

In the first year of his online program, Mike was able to take four weeks of winter vacation and still accomplish all the required studying during vacation. He could not have done all this, and earned excellent grades in his online courses, without developing excellent study skills. Mike's advice: "Every online student can do what I did, but it takes commitment, organization, and time management to survive!"

Thomas E. Escott, MSEd, began his teaching career in Boston, where he taught seventh- and eighth-grade math from 1973 to 1977. After four years, he decided to enter the rapidly expanding computer field, where he then spent twenty-five years in various positions: programmer, technical support, technical writer, and network manager. All of these positions involved helping and teaching others. After twenty-five years, Tom realized that he had never stopped being a teacher and so he returned to the classroom in 2003, this time at the high school level. From the first year, he infused all his lessons with technology.

In 2007, Tom received a master's degree in education with a focus on integrating technology in the classroom, an online program through Walden University. Most recently, he has been facilitating math courses in three virtual high schools and has tutored elementary students online. Tom's advice: "Thanks to the growing opportunities for online education, I am now living my dream of teaching other teachers online. You can reach your dreams, too, through online learning."

Sara Bender, MS, obtained a bachelor's degree in psychology and then entered the field of mental health. She found a passion for working with the chronically mentally ill, including those diagnosed with schizophrenia, bipolar disorder, and other illnesses. She quickly learned, however, that advancement and obtaining a license required a graduate degree. Sara found an online program that allowed her the flexibility of maintaining her current career while going to school.

After obtaining her graduate degree, Sara taught an introduction to psychology course on campus and found the experience thrilling. In time, she pursued additional teaching opportunities and is currently teaching courses both in a traditional classroom and online. Sara's advice: "Whatever the reason for a person's return to the classroom, I believe that the instructor and student, collaboratively, are responsible for the student's ability to consider new ideas, challenge previously held beliefs, and overall success in the course."

Breinigsville, PA USA
14 December 2010
251411BV00001B/2/P

9 781607 097471